RESTORING
the
GOOD
SOCIETY

Praise for *Restoring the Good Society*

"Don Eberly has written a provocative and convicting book that explains a great deal about how and why America is going off the rails. More important, he advances credible proposals for American renewal. It's one of the best books I've read this year; I recommend it highly."
—William L. Armstrong, former U.S. Senator

"Don Eberly pinpoints the source of America's social ills. It's not politics or economics. It's moral decline. And the answer lies not in Washington but in local institutions—the church, schools, community groups, families. This is a timely, persuasive book."
—Fred Barnes, *The New Republic*

"*Restoring the Good Society* is an important book that deals with important matters. The American people should read it, reflect on it, and act on it. Our future will be brighter if they do."
—William J. Bennett

"A superb blend of sanity, savvy, and groundbreaking courage, Eberly's vision and proposals deserve wide consideration. They point the way forward out of the impasse of the culture wars."
—Os Guinness, author of *The American Hour*

"Don Eberly cogently summarizes the major cultural and political challenges facing American public life and outlines a thoughtful and realistic strategy of action. *Restoring the Good Society* could very well mark a turning point in evangelical thinking about American public life."
—James Davison Hunter, author of *Culture Wars*

"Don Eberly has written a timely, persuasive, important book on the limits of politics and the limitless potential of families, neighborhoods, and individuals to reconstruct our 'moral infrastructure.' In the process, he pushes beyond the bitterness of America's cultural conflicts to a hopeful vision that will challenge and inspire both left and right."
—Jack Kemp

"Don Eberly offers a well-informed, thoughtful, and morally bracing call for the renewal of the American experiment, beginning with ourselves. Christians and others will have their courage and imagination challenged by engaging this important argument."
—Richard John Neuhaus, Editor-in-chief, *First Things*

Don E. Eberly

Restoring *the* Good Society

A New Vision for Politics and Culture

Foreword by William J. Bennett

HOURGLASS BOOKS

Baker Books

A Division of Baker Book House Co
Grand Rapids, Michigan 49516

ISBN 0-8010-3226-1

Printed in the United States of America

Cover by Multnomah Graphics

Library of Congress Cataloging-in-Publication Data

Eberly, Don E.
    Restoring the good society : a new vision for politics and culture
/ Don E. Eberly
        p.   cm.
    Includes bibliographical references.
    ISBN 0-8010-3226-1
    1. Religion and politics—United States. 2. Values—Political
aspects—United States. 3. Social ethics. I. Title.
BL65.P7E24   1993
261'.0973—dc20   93-48973

Nothing that is worth doing can be achieved in our lifetime; therefore we must be saved by hope. Nothing which is true or beautiful or good makes complete sense in any immediate context of history; therefore we must be saved by faith. Nothing we do, however virtuous, can be accomplished alone; therefore we are saved by love. No virtuous act is quite as virtuous from the standpoint of our friend or foe as it is from our standpoint. Therefore we must be saved by the final form of love which is forgiveness.

—Reinhold Niebuhr

All we have willed or hoped or dreamed of good shall exist;
Not its semblance, but itself; no beauty, nor good, nor power
Whose voice has gone forth, but each survives for the melodist
When eternity affirms the conception of an hour.
The high that proved too high, the heroic for earth too hard,
The passion that left the ground to lose itself in the sky;
Are music sent up to heaven by the lover and the bard;
Enough that he heard it once: we shall hear it by-and-by.

—from "Abt Vogler" by Robert Browning

CONTENTS

ACKNOWLEDGMENTS

People are said to be the product of two things: their friends and their books. I acknowledge my debt to both. For the great authors throughout history who inspire me: C. S. Lewis, St. Augustine, Leo Tolstoy, Edmund Burke, T. S. Eliot, Fyodor Dostoyevsky, Jacques Ellul, Reinhold and Richard Niebuhr, Christopher Dawson, Dietrich Bonhoeffer, and John Courtney Murray.

For contemporary writers who have lifted my living and leading to a higher plane: Peter Berger and his unique understanding of culture; Robert Bellah, who shows the importance of community; Paul Johnson, who penetrates the currents of history; Richard John Neuhaus, who practices the integrated faith; and Aleksandr Solzhenitsyn, the great living monument to spiritual triumph over evil.

And for two remarkable leaders for whom I have been fortunate to work, Ronald Reagan and Jack Kemp, who remain incorrigibly cheerful about America. I also owe a significant debt of gratitude to Os Guinness, whose gift of brilliance has profited me enormously.

As to friends, the most cherished of all are family. To kids a father could only dream of having, Preston, Caroline, and Margaret, and to my friend and partner who is my wife, Sheryl, I owe all that I have gained in adulthood.

Thanks too to friends: to Peb Jackson, who always encourages; to Myron Stoltzfus, Mike Landis, and Jim Martin; to several who reviewed and improved the manuscript, long-time friend Frank Gregorsky and Dean Curry; to competent staffers Wendy Lentvorsky, Keith Bashore, Charles Greenawalt, and Cliff Frick; and to the ablest of editors a neophyte writer could ever hope to have, Amy Boucher.

FOREWORD

RESTORING THE GOOD SOCIETY makes a valuable contribution to the public debate because it does something that we too rarely see these days: it engages serious moral issues in a morally serious way.

Don Eberly's work begins with a premise: something has gone wrong at the core of modern American society. During the last three decades, we have seen exploding rates in social pathologies: enormous increases in murder and violent crime, out-of-wedlock births, abortions, divorces, teen suicides, and a severe decline in educational achievement. These have taken an enormous human toll, in terms of wasted, shattered, and lost lives.

The problems are serious. But we should not despair. What we need to do is to get smart and fight back, for the sake of our children. We need to push hard against an age that is pushing very hard against us.

The solution to the trials of our time depends on replenishing America's moral capital. It has been depleted by the failure of our character-forming institutions to carry out their time-honored tasks. Cultural renewal depends above all on strengthening and revitalizing our social institutions: families, churches and synagogues, schools, neighborhoods, and civic associations.

Social and cultural renewal will require the mobilization of citizens and leaders across all sectors of American life. It will require restoring professions, creating a new citizenship guided by common-sense problem solving at the neighborhood level, and fostering a new spirit of community that seeks to repair our culture's declining civility and order.

Restoring the Good Society also reminds us of the limits of public policies. Human happiness is linked to more than good government; it requires a culture committed to nourishing the soul of human beings, not just their appetites.

The last quarter-century has taught politicians a hard and humbling lesson: there are intrinsic limits to what the state can do, particularly when it comes to imparting virtue, forming and forging character, and providing peace to souls. Samuel Johnson expressed this sentiment when he wrote, "How small, of all that human hearts endure, That part which laws or kings can cause or cure!"

Politics is a great adventure; it is greatly important; but its proper place in our lives has been greatly exaggerated. Politics—especially inside the Beltway politics—has too often become the graven image of our time.

Here is one of the hard truths that offends the modern age; not only are there some tasks that government cannot do, in a nation of free and sovereign people, there are some tasks that government should not do. The American experiment, after all, depends both upon the capacity of individuals to govern themselves as well as on a measure of civic virtue.

In *Restoring the Good Society*, Don Eberly describes America's cultural crisis; the diminishing power of politics to solve our most pressing social problems; and delivers a broad, hopeful vision for the renewal of American society—for recreating "the good society."

These are impressive achievements. But there is something else impressive as well: in a sometimes contentious debate about social and cultural issues, Don Eberly adds a calm, civilized, and reasoned voice.

Restoring the Good Society is an important book that deals with important matters. The American people should read it, reflect on it, and act on it. Our future will be brighter if they do.

—William J. Bennett
Washington, D.C.

1

THE SEARCH FOR AMERICA'S LOST SOUL

AS WE NEAR THE END of a century and a millennium, America is entering a collective search for its national soul. The country is experiencing profound changes in demographics, economics, and technology. The great projects that stirred nationalist spirits in the past—whether settling frontiers, defeating international communism, or launching "great societies"—have either been accomplished or were tried and failed.

These and other factors are producing a ferment in public life that has yet to be fully understood or tapped. As politics continues to be absorbed in its own reality, Americans are steadily understanding that the quality of life for many is declining, and that the economy and national politics is not as influential as many politicians or members of the media regularly suggest.

Self-doubt is a new and strange experience for America, a nation more self-assured in its mission and confident of its destiny than perhaps any ever to exist. Yet Americans are groping to overcome this new crisis of self-confidence and are in the midst of a search for meaning and purpose in public life.

The debate for the balance of this decade, and perhaps well into the next century, will focus on a modern paradox: How can a society that has produced more freedom and prosperity than any other in history, and has been so generous in its distribution, also increasingly lead the world in many categories of social pathology?

Many realize that politics alone has not effected what Americans prize the most—a humane and civilized society. Secularism has not supplied a sense of meaning and purpose to public life in America; sectarianism has framed spiritual restoration almost entirely in terms of politics and power. Secularists and sectarians alike have come to understand and explain social reality in the context of power, and thus have resisted attempts to transcend politics and join the urgent mission of restoring the good society.

The good society is a society with shared values and personal and social order. It consists of positive ideals, strong communities, civility, and manners. It can neither be doled out as just another entitlement, nor pieced together through programs, nor stimulated into existence by tax cuts. Instead it must be achieved through the cooperative efforts of individuals from all sectors of society.

To restore the good society conventional politics will need to give way to new coalitions and themes that emphasize the quality of life in the context of neighborhood. Those themes should include a "new citizenship" that views individuals as the agents of change, a "new localism" that expands the capacity of the institutions closest to the people to solve problems, and a "new familism" that sees effective parenting as the only true solution in protecting children from the ravages of a hostile culture.

THE DEATH OF OLD IDEAS

America is in the midst of a major upheaval that may only occur every several hundred years. What lies immediately ahead for America's citizens, institutions, and patterns of life is less clear than what is passing: the politics, ideologies, and major intellectual currents of much of the twentieth century. According to futurist William Van Dusen Wishard,

> All the major currents of twentieth-century intellectual thought have now dried up. Marxism has collapsed. Socialism is vanishing. Totalitarianism is discredited. Even the French are losing faith in rationalism. Liberalism inspires few hearts

and little action. . . . Modernism has deconstructed. While science continues unabated, few believe that the objectivity of science provides ultimate meaning in life.[1]

All of this leaves us groping for authority and legitimacy in the body politic and for some transcendental belief in society at large.

In response to this upheaval, conservative thinker Irving Kristol has predicted a closing of the age of secularism and a resurgence of faith. "In the decades ahead, the decline of secularism will signify the decline of liberalism as well. Already on the fringes of liberalism itself, artists and philosophers are welcoming the collapse of a 'secular humanism' they find sterile and oppressive."[2]

With this collapse Kristol sees a coming new "conservative century." But others are not so sure. Many doubt that conservatism, as currently constituted, will rise from the ashes of secular liberalism's demise. Although liberalism has failed to reverse "the unraveling of the social fabric" through the welfare state, historian Christopher Lasch notes that conservatism has failed to "answer the aspiration of community" because it ignores "the corrosive effects of capitalism itself."[3]

In other words, neither the welfare state nor a surging capitalism has solved many of society's persistent problems; in fact, each has contributed in its own way to the corrosion of civil society and its institutions. When the mediating structures of society—families, churches, communities, and voluntary associations—are weakened to the breaking point, individuals are increasingly left isolated and vulnerable before an ever expanding state. Neither the conservative mantra of "more markets" nor the liberal song of stronger "safety nets" in an expanded state is adequate.

But modernity, more so than politics, has produced much of society's fragmentation and rootlessness. Sociologist Daniel Bell has described modernity as "a rage against order," meaning a steady undermining of voluntary institutions and restraints. And Catholic political theorist David Walsh has characterized the modern period by "driving passions for self-salvation, faith in the limitless power of technology," and "supreme confidence in the unending possibilities of industrial, social and political progress."[4]

Bell, Walsh, and others have issued warnings against an overconfidence in the power of human beings. Writing in 1978, Bell predicted the slow end of an era: "The exhaustion of Modernism, the aridity of Communist life, the tedium of the unrestrained self, and the meaninglessness of the monolithic political chants, all indicate that a long era is coming to a slow close."[5]

What alternative vision of order can replace modernity's commitment to human omnipotence? Perhaps a deep ideological exhaustion has finally set in; perhaps the more honest shapers of culture will have to admit the limitations of the power of human beings to dominate and define reality according to their own purposes.

That framework may not have been invented yet. To break out of the existing fixation with Washington public policy strategies, new political and social movements will need to emerge to promote national renewal. Sociologist Robert Bellah and others have issued calls for a new politics and debate that balances the existing language of individualism with an understanding of the older traditions of biblical religion, classical philosophy, and civic republicanism. The public philosophy of this new movement would be, in Bellah's words, "less trapped in the clichés of rugged individualism" and "more open to an invigorating, fulfilling sense of social responsibility."[6]

What shape will the era immediately ahead take? Will it be a continuing expansion of the secular welfare state fueled by a desperately determined political liberalism? Will it be a conservatism driven by a resurgence of religious forces? Will it be the communitarian's vision? Or will it be some synthesis of these philosophical currents yet to be created? The dominant ideas of the twentieth century, having powerful allies and a deep residue in the culture, will not just disappear. But there could be a sudden shift that produces a search for spiritual truth and transcendence as intense as the twentieth century's search for scientific truth.

As more Americans are thinking about matters personal, spiritual, and relational, there will be a renewed interest in building a stronger society. Perhaps the next century will bring a new spiritual reformation that empowers individuals to do the work of God in restoring families, rebuilding cities, and renewing community. Perhaps a determined effort will be made to free people from a client status in a paternalistic state and to restore values of individual responsibility and respect. Whatever the outcome, it is clear that new political or public policy strategies alone will not suffice.

THE DECLINE OF POLITICS

Politics inspires little confidence today because our cultural disorder has produced problems that lie largely beyond the capacity of government to solve. Administrations come and go, promising much but accomplishing little more than minor tinkering with bureaucracy, programs, and tax and criminal codes. The government and the economy are too large, and the country's problems too complex, for public policy tools to make a significant difference.

Yet public policy professionals maintain an unshakable confidence in their technical remedies. As Bellah has observed, it is tempting to think that "the problems that we face today, from the homeless in the streets and poverty in the Third World to ozone depletion and the greenhouse effect, can be solved by technology or technical expertise alone."[7]

As the nation's expert class chatters on with its own language of arcane governmentalism, the people are given fewer reasons to stay tuned. For the foreseeable future, academics and policy professionals will be asked more frequently to document the failures of public programs than to map believable new strategies. Addressing the same problems over and over again without meaningful results eventually turns the political process into "a cruel, repetitious bore."[8]

Those who simplistically think the answer to America's problems is finding "another Reagan" to launch for political office should be sobered by an assessment of the immediate past. For it was during the roaring eighties, with exploding economic growth, surging patriotism, and confidence-boosting successes in foreign policy, that the cultural indicators—illegitimacy, drugs, crime, and educational decline—either remained stagnant or accelerated southward. Although the nation's self-confidence may have been momentarily restored in cultural terms, the eighties were anything but "morning again in America." The best policy proposals could not reduce crime and drugs or reverse the decline in families and neighborhoods. No amount of stirring pro-family rhetoric could reverse the coarsening of America's popular culture.

There is little evidence that the eighties was a time of deepening conservatism, except that people preferred less generous aid to the poor, more protection from crime, and less tolerance of social engineering in such forms as busing and affirmative action. In other words, this was an era whose conservatism may have been defined as much by self-interest as by lofty ideals. For much of the American public, social values remained largely unchanged. In fact, one could argue that the cultural values of the sixties, particularly the sexual revolution, continued; we simply added the value of getting rich. Many thought the country was becoming more conservative because her sons and daughters were pursuing degrees in business, not social work.

In terms of morality, the eighties was a decade in which much of society, rich and poor alike, sang off the same sheet of music. Those at the top extolled wealth and skirted ethics: taxpayers doled out billions in a Savings-and-Loan bailout to cover the escapades of junk-bond billionaires. At the bottom, welfare expenditures could not be reduced as social programs were forced to accommodate rising illegitimacy and welfare dependence.

Optimistic budget forecasts had to be repeatedly revised, and the national debt skyrocketed.

The 1980s represented a flowering of the American conservative movement. For eight years, Ronald Reagan—who delivered the nominating speech for Barry Goldwater in 1964—brought to the most powerful office and the most powerful bully pulpit in the world the most powerful communication skills of perhaps any president in the twentieth century. Few can deny that much was accomplished: the judiciary was reformed, a reformed tax structure fueled a vast expansion in the economy, America's long struggle with totalitarianism was successfully concluded in the demise of the Soviet Union, the steep upward slope in spending trends was moderated, and the drift in the culture toward libertine values found some resistance in Reagan's social policy.

But the eighties simply did not provide the social and moral renewal that many had longed for. It was during the feel-good eighties, for example, that single-parent households increased by 40 percent. The rise of AIDS, rather than halting the sexual revolution as might have been expected, provided the pretext for graphic sex education and new homosexual power. For the first time in American history, families were raising children amidst open discussion of sexual disease and sexual practices politely termed "alternative lifestyles." The decade dominated by Reagan and the politics of the Moral Majority was a decade that ended with American culture more drenched in sexual themes than ever.

Politics is now courting declining relevance. For one, the debate now consists of battles over whose experts and whose policies can solve problems that are inherently behavioral, and thus often beyond the capacity of public policy to solve. Secular experts, trained in the tools of the empirical sciences but frequently bereft of any meaningful association with values and vision, are left to mutter about mechanistic theories. After clumsy attempts to debate values backfired, paralyzed politicians now quietly slip through the rear exits of the vexing territory of values, returning to the safer terrain of such vapid slogans as "It's the economy stupid."

And neither the political Right nor the Left have restored the moral order of society. Lasch has described a "baffled sense of drift" on the political Right, in spite of its record of "successes." "The New Right came to power with a mandate not just to free the market from bureaucratic interferences but to halt the slide into apathy, hedonism and moral chaos. It has not lived up to expectations."[9] The perception of spiritual disrepair is just as evident today in spite of the Right's deference to traditional values. Lasch believes this is because the Right operates on many of the same assumptions as the Left: the belief in acquisitive individualism and "the desirability and inevitability of technical and economic development."[10]

The coming debate will surely focus on the quality of life, with public policy recognized more for its limitations than its achievements. This is not to say that public policy in a host of moral and economic policy areas is unimportant. In dozens of areas, whether on social issues, education, regulation, or taxation, policy makers will determine how much of Americans' earnings the citizens will get to keep, how individuals can create and dispose of their wealth, and most importantly, whose values are reflected in judicial and legislative policy. These deeply important matters cannot be avoided by those concerned for the direction of America.

But it is equally true that the quality of life in our families and neighborhoods is not likely to improve until society comes to grips collectively with the root causes of America's decline: the steady decay in individual manners and morals.

A NEW AMERICAN RESTORATION MOVEMENT

It is time to organize a new American restoration movement. The focus should not be on political ideology or partisanship, but instead on an all-fronts mobilization of individual Americans to improve the social and moral infrastructure of America.

The movement must attempt to forge a new consensus on the basic values upon which a free society rests: values almost entirely embodied in the concepts of respect and responsibility.

The restoration of America will begin within each individual. And so we must enlist leadership from all sectors of society to rebuild American greatness around the tripod of character, community, and culture. The mission of the business and professional community should be ethics and quality. The focus of education should be character and classical virtue. The effort of politics should be to restore the integrity and competence of our public institutions.

The chief priorities in the realm of religion should be to resist the power option in order to serve hungry souls and desecularize public life. Public leaders must strive to legitimate again religion's influence in shaping society's mores. America remains one of the most incorrigibly religious nations on earth, according to many opinion polls. Contrary to some people's expectations and wishes, it is religion's secular foes, not religion itself, that emerges weakened after many decades of head-to-head conflict.

Yet organized religion, both the institutional church and the hundreds of entrepreneurial organizations it has spawned, does not face a new century unscathed. It has suffered serious wounds—some self-inflicted, some from the determined attempts by its foes to secularize America, and some simply due to the corrosive and relativizing effects of modernity that it has done little to resist. There are few signs that traditional religious institutions—now highly commercialized and committed to the same measurements of success as non-religious institutions—stand poised to play the central, undisputed role they once enjoyed in shaping the values of society.

To promote the good society, we will need to undertake five key steps. The first is to *realize that much of American life must become less politicized.* The uniquely American forms of extremism that Alexis de Tocqueville warned about—materialism and individualism—are producing a democratic "despotism" that insists that all conflicts and disagreements be resolved by asserting power. It will certainly not be easy to move beyond a pre-occupation with power and rights in a society dominated for several decades by a radical individualism of both the Left and the Right. The attempts of many today to attach legal status to every passion and impulse has divided Americans into warring mobs. This division makes the restoration of community, perhaps the deepest of all current yearnings, almost impossible.

The second step is to *learn to value values*. Instead of abandoning the values debate because of those who abuse it through rhetorical overkill, we must reframe and refocus the debate. The anxiety about public and private morality runs across the political spectrum, and there is much at stake for everyone, particularly children, regardless of religion or ideology. We must intelligently explain the relationship of declining values to many of society's pressing problems—its litigiousness, declining competitiveness, runaway public entitlements, special-interest politics, and the insatiable demand for more rights.

The third step in promoting the good society is to *broaden the discussion of values beyond the domain of political ideology and sectarian religion*. The current debate in America concerns the kind of society that all of us, liberal or conservative, must live in. America needs a new language to talk about values that transcends cultural and religious boundaries. Whatever else the family-values debate may be, it must be primarily about valuing the family and seeking to preserve it.

The fourth step is to *realize that social and cultural renewal is about changing people, not just government*. Therefore we need methods aimed at persuasion, not imposition. Traditionalists would do well to promote the conservative values of moderation and a strong commitment to democratic pluralism. The majority of Americans are tolerant traditionalists who are weary of having to choose between the equally unpalatable choices of either extreme secularism or extreme moralism.

And the fifth step is to *understand that the debate about values is not merely a debate over single issues*. Though important, the difficult battles over abortion, homosexuality, and dozens of other moral issues should be viewed as symptoms of a deeper disorder: the complete triumph of rights over responsibilities and of self-expression over self-sublimation. If "manners are more important than laws" (Edmund Burke), why should we be surprised that homosexuality would emerge from the closet in search of public acceptance in a society that no longer minds its manners in heterosexual conduct? This is not said to minimize or relativize the moral issues that deeply divide Americans. But those who would exploit these great divides while ignoring the need to bind up the nation's wounds may be tearing apart the very social fabric they believe their actions are protecting.

America finds itself once again in the midst of deep social conflict. Some would call it culture wars. A society is in trouble not only when it has lost its sense of internal order and equilibrium—its cultural authority—but when it attempts to reestablish authority through political power only provoke and exacerbate the conflict.

America will be saved one family, one neighborhood, one school at a time—from the bottom up. Few of America's vast non-ideological middle believe that government run by either the Left or Right will make much of a difference. This does not mean that individuals have any less responsibility to exercise their political responsibilities; it only means that legislative change must be accompanied by broad-based change in values and conduct at the personal level. We must move beyond public policy to personal policy.

2

THE SOCIAL ROOTS OF AMERICAN DISORDER

A CRITICAL PART of America's national cohesion comes from the ideas and values that are embodied and preserved in America's basic institutions. Many wonder if America as we know it can exist without a shared commitment to such basic values and ideas as self-restraint, sacrifice, and respect for the common good. These shared ideas are reborn and buttressed in every great exertion of national resolve, whether in striking out against domestic poverty, winning foreign wars, defeating international communism, or exploring the frontiers of space. With these projects either accomplished and behind us or languishing, Americans now read newspaper headlines that tell a story of grim reality at home.

The search for explanations for America's deepening disorder is not confined to editorial pages or academic journals. Warnings of a "social meltdown" have been coming from those working on the front lines of America's social agencies, schools and universities, think tanks, and courts. The message of alarm, whether emanating from cities, suburbs, or the smallest hamlets in America, has the same content and tone.

Those who are issuing the warnings see the relationship between private morality and the quality of public life. Societies that become indifferent to this relationship face negative social and economic consequences. People are growing aware that what America has come to celebrate the most—untrammeled moral freedom for individuals—has come at a cost to our common culture and institutions. The resulting loss of morality has weakened the family and other social institutions, leading to increased crime and poverty.

THE WEAKENED FAMILY

In no category has the declining quality of our culture and behavior been more devastating than on America's children. For example, since 1960 divorce rates have doubled, the annual suicide rate for teenagers has tripled, and births to unwed mothers have risen from 5 percent to nearly 30 percent of all births (and dramatically higher in many cities). The sexual and physical abuse of children has tripled over twenty years, with 2.5 million kids now subjected to it every year. Estimates for the number of homeless children range from two hundred twenty thousand to seven hundred fifty thousand.

For the children of African-Americans, the outlook has become even bleaker. Black America is in a crisis of poverty, crime, drugs, and disintegration. Black children have double the infant mortality rate of whites and are three times more likely to live in single-parent households. Forty-three percent of all African-American children live in poverty.

Children are dramatically worse off today than in previous generations—in spite of record prosperity, jobs, and expenditures for social services. Possibly no other generation of young people in an affluent country has been made so vulnerable to social and psychological risks associated with having parents that are dysfunctional, divorced, or simply disinterested.

The cultural freedoms of recent decades have conferred upon adults permission to divorce with ease as they assure themselves that their children are "resilient." Only now is the practice beginning to be challenged as social research yields new information to indicate that children have unmistakably been the losers. Research shows that children from broken homes are more likely to fail in school, drop out, develop behavioral and emotional disorders, engage in early sex, get pregnant, fail in their own marriages—if they get married at all—and pass on these same patterns to their own children.

The language of deficits, once applied only to fiscal short-falls, is now applied to families to describe the lack of adequate parenting and character development. A deficit of fathering exists for the one in four children who are now born each year without the benefit of two parents, and for the many more who will spend a portion of their childhood with only one parent. For two-parent, double-career households, there is a deficit in time. Not surprisingly, there is also a serious deficit in the material circumstances of millions of American children living in poverty.

The debate about saving the family remains gridlocked in a tug of war over what the government should do—how much and in what form—or not do. This impoverished debate serves to reinforce the positions of the organizations and antagonists on each opposing side. But efforts to strengthen the family should not depend on the outcome of a debate over taxes, incentives, and welfare. The family unit will be made important again when Americans decide to promote and secure it in all sectors of society; when Americans decide that the revolutions in sexual conduct and divorce have gone too far; when it is socially important once more to be "a good family man."

CRIME AND TAXPAYER PUNISHMENT

The most intractable and costly social problem in America may be crime. As the makeup of the prison population demonstrates, crime is frequently a direct outcome of the weakening of the family and other social institutions. Family scholar Barbara Dafoe Whitehead has said that the relationship between crime and one-parent families is so strong that "controlling for family configuration erases the relationship between race and crime and between low income and crime."[1] Seventy percent of the occupants of juvenile detention centers are from fatherless families.

Per capital spending on prisons has increased 400 percent over the past twenty years. In the 1980s alone, America spent $30 billion to double its prison capacity.[2] Over a million Americans go to sleep behind bars—more than any nation, with only South Africa and the former Soviet Union coming close.

Like so many other social policy debates, the debate about crime is governed more by partisan needs than a grounding in reality. Political promises to reduce crime focus mostly on the need to "lock 'em up." This assumes that Americans are willing to pay any price for any amount of prison space.

But the governors, mayors, and police department chiefs who receive these funds privately indicate that no amount of increased money or personnel will be sufficient to stem the tide of crime. Dismissing crime as a function of too few convictions and too few convicts behind bars is a convenient path for politicians to follow. Of course there is some truth to this argument, just as there is also some truth to the other argument that crime is the result of joblessness, poverty, and illiteracy.

None of these factors by themselves, however, come close to telling the whole story of why crime does or does not exist in society. These explanations do not follow the evidence of history. The crime rate was not as high during earlier periods of economic dislocation in America, nor is crime nearly as high today among other countries whose per capita wealth is only a fraction of ours.

James Q. Wilson, a leading crime expert, has written extensively on the root causes of crime. Wilson searched for correlations between outbursts of criminal violence and economic deprivation. It was paradoxically during the times of economic dislocation—the industrial revolution, rapid urbanization at the turn of the century, and the Great Depression—that crime significantly decreased. Wilson found that crime is, in large measure, not a function of money, but rather of changing morality. Crime will not be significantly reduced until the institutions that impart faith, character, and self-restraint—particularly the institution of the family—are rebuilt.

Crime is particularly ravaging the black community. Socializing young males—a serious challenge for any society—is especially difficult here as 68 percent of the children are now born to father-absent households. Homicide is the leading cause of death for African-American males between the ages of 15 and 44. In 1989, 23 percent of African-American males in this age group were either in prison, on probation, or on parole.[3]

A growing number of African-American scholars and journalists are concluding that dramatic changes must come from within their community. For instance, Washington Post columnist William Raspberry calls for a renewed focus on the internal enemy of crime—family dissolution and despair. He calls for a "save the children crusade" that would flood urban schools and neighborhoods with mentors and tutors. Though material resources are needed, the great need is for people of all colors "to grasp the hand of every child that reaches out for help."[4]

AMERICA'S POVERTY OF CULTURE AND CULTURE OF POVERTY

Author George Gilder has said that if Americans did three basic things, they would have less than 1 percent chance of living in poverty: graduate from high school, get married and stay married, take a job, any job, and keep it. Poverty in America, particularly how long it lasts, is a function of a person's decisions in the area of education, family, and work ethic.

If behavioral reforms were promoted, the gap between rich and poor would be substantially narrowed and American society would be more just and fair. According to the National Commission on Children, chaired by Senator Jay Rockefeller, although only 7 percent of two-parent families are poor, 43 percent of mother-only families live below the official poverty level. The number of single-parent families has doubled over the past twenty years, with 43 percent of these households living in poverty.[5]

No one chooses poverty, but individual value decisions, particularly behaviors that risk pregnancy, strongly affect one's social and economic status. Along with policy recommendations, the Rockefeller commission report offers a straightforward value statement as well, as if to acknowledge the limits of political and governmental solutions. Rather than calling for dramatically expanded social welfare programs, it recommends behavioral reform, specifically for "delaying pregnancy until parents are financially and emotionally capable of assuming the obligations of parenthood."[6]

Poverty has always existed, and if history is any guide, always will. What is different about today's poverty is the sense of its never-ending permanence. This chips away at one of America's most cherished ideals: the promise of upward mobility. American relief, which was first offered as a temporary way station for families caught in tough transitions, has become the final destination for many. The bulk of Aid to Families with Dependent Children (AFDC) expenditures now goes to covering female parents who spend eight years or longer on the program. Forty-five-year-old great grandmothers are now common, with children having children in their early teens, often by choice.

Many of the theories about welfare dependence focus on a welfare system's distorted incentives instead of the nation's distorted values. But the evidence suggests that the latter is closer to the truth. The rise of many of today's notorious urban problems—illegitimacy, crime, declining educational achievement, and work avoidance—accompanied, and in some cases preceded, the rise of the welfare state. Moreover, many of these social pathologies also took root among the non-poor during the same time period, but to a lesser extent. The likelier explanation for the changing character of American poverty is the changing character of American culture.

Concerns regarding the self-perpetuating qualities of welfare were first voiced by "culture of poverty" theorists. The poor are mired in poverty, according to the theory, because they have developed a distinct and separate value system; it is a culture alienated from mainstream values. This hypothesis is plausible for understanding and explaining the kind of long-term poverty that has been targeted again and again for elimination. But this analysis can easily degenerate into a new variant of "blaming the victim," which mostly serves to exonerate the middle and upper classes who pay the bill.

Although this theory may help explain poverty, it fails to account for the changing values of the so-called "mainstream." The poor, for instance, are said to be sexually irresponsible. But a deterioration in mainstream middle-class society over the past twenty years has been a determining factor in society's sexual behavior, according to the National Academy of Science.[7]

Another view this theory embraces is that poor people have a low view of family. Although rates of family instability and non-formation are certainly greater among the poor than the non-poor, the United States as a whole leads the world in divorce. And out-of-wedlock births have recently risen almost as rapidly among the middle class as among the poor. It is clear that not only the poor exercise a low commitment to the family. Still another view is that the poor are said to be incapable of deferring gratification. But the poor are not alone, as cultural forces of self-gratification and conspicuous consumption have affected behavior across all income groups.

The headline-grabbing stories of urban mayhem are not the real story of scandal in America. Our nation's dirty little secret involves the state of the middle-class culture, a culture consisting predominantly of quiet suburbs. If accurately told, one would read a sordid account of drugs, youth alcoholism, sexual promiscuity, and dysfunctional families. The difference is that kids resolve their crisis pregnancies by aborting their unborn, they consume drugs and alcohol at private parties under the tacit consent of parents and police, and their delinquency is conveniently swept under the rug of middle-class respectability.

In other words, the "moral" difference between the poor and everyone else may be less conspicuous than assumed. The problem with the poor is not that they have developed their own set of values, but that they have failed to do so. To make it out of poverty, the poor may have to rely more heavily than non-poor Americans on rugged values of work, sacrifice, family, and community.

Until recent decades, America's middle and upper class considered it their social duty to nourish character and responsibility among the poor. Previously the upper classes did so more easily because they lived in close proximity to the lower class, shared in the life of the community, and modeled the values they voiced. This explains why so many in the older generations recall being raised with little money but without knowing they were poor—they were rich in character and dignity.

Today's urban restoration will neither come primarily from the financial generosity of the welfare state nor from a newly sympathetic middle class. Breaking the bondage of dependency will require more than introducing economic opportunity or eliminating welfare. True restoration comes from developing the inner resources of urban residents. And this is what political leadership should aim to do.

Indeed, spiritual renewal, which has sustained people in the face of overwhelming odds in the past, is the key to social and economic renewal. To reduce poverty, values-shaping institutions must place a new emphasis on faith, family, enterprise formation, rugged self-help, and a new interdependence within neighborhoods. The government alone will not be able to rescue urban families and children, as growing numbers of urban leaders are beginning to recognize.

That the government is out of answers for these deep social problems is no justification for citizens to be out of compassion. It only supplies a mandate for direct personal involvement and creative strategies for cooperative action to rebuild America. For true American restoration will not be effected by politics alone, but rather through cultural change.

3

CULTURE AND THE POLITICS OF VALUES

IDEAS AND VALUES have powerful consequences. The power of ideas in politics is often oversold, but the power of basic ideas and assumptions in the culture is rarely fully appreciated. Culture consists of the basic beliefs, ideas, and values of a people that shape and define individual lives. H. Richard Niebuhr described culture as the "work of men's minds and hands."[1] It is reflected in speech, education, myth, science, art, philosophy, government, law, rite, beliefs, inventions, and technologies.

Cultural institutions are deeply influential in shaping the direction of a society. High culture consists of the world of the universities and the arts, including the debate among the policy and academic professionals and the writers and commentators who offer analysis and opinion. Popular culture includes entertainment, film, and popular books and literature.

High and popular culture is shaped and defined within a free flow of ideas and values. Whether future observers judge the late twentieth century as a period in which Americans searched for higher meaning or was a time of cultural and moral decline will be determined more by the themes and symbols of culture than by the country's political debate.

What cultural shifts have occurred during the past thirty years? At the level of elite culture, there has been an almost diabolical determination to weaken the influence of such basic institutions as the family and faith in American society. At the level

34

of mass culture, the entertainment industry flooded American homes with programming of mind-numbing banality, which has trivialized life and desensitized Americans to the deepening disorder. It seems that American popular culture has ceased to feel any responsibility for elevating and ennobling Americans.

The cultural history Americans are currently writing reveals an ugly picture for a society so enlightened. One in ten children is reported to have fired a gun at another person by the twelfth grade;[2] sexual activity now begins at ten and eleven years of age for many children (in 1992 the number of those who gave birth under the age of fourteen was fourteen thousand); gangs of boys measure their manhood by the number of girls they have bedded—frequently by force; rape, violence, and assaults on teachers are so commonplace they often go unreported. But even these anti-social behaviors are rooted in deeper societal changes that have broadened the parameters of acceptable opinion and behavior to a degree that would not have been sanctioned even a decade ago.

CULTURAL REFORMATION BRINGS LASTING LEGISLATIVE CHANGE

This drift in culture has not emanated from the lawmaking bodies of cities, states, or the federal government; it has been produced by the idea shapers who work at the vital center of the nation's cultural life. For ideas and values are likely to have their most powerful impact in the realm of culture, not in the political realm. Most Americans cannot name their state legislators, or even their U.S. Representatives, much less pattern their lives after legislative pronouncements and initiatives. But individuals are deeply influenced by a popular culture that flows like a torrent into their lives through radio, television, film, MTV, talk shows, pulp novels, magazines, and newspapers.

Government is not and cannot be the primary source of culture formation. Similarly, politics is a weak and often inappropriate instrument for solving problems that are inherently cultural, moral, and spiritual. Many subscribe to the populist fallacy that cultural disorder will be solved when a few more activists are driven into the streets, a new dream candidate is discovered and elected, and bad laws are replaced by good laws.

There are no revolutionary ideas in politics today, which itself is a revolutionary idea. Very few solutions will be found in legal change, new administrative techniques, or large-scale government reforms. When people recognize this, they become free to direct some of their energies elsewhere. Politics becomes peripheral, rather than central, to our neighborhoods and families.

American renewal will come as much from outside of politics as within it. Although politics is important, it has little restorative power in itself. For a nation's public life to be regenerated, the spirit and mind of individual citizens must be renewed first. Without changes in the cultural ethos, lasting legislative change can be elusive; what is won today can be reversed tomorrow, and often is. The deeper social currents that operate below the surface of politics are likely to have more of a lasting effect.

William Wilberforce—the great nineteenth-century British statesman who fought the British slave trade against extremely difficult odds over a lifetime in the Parliament—understood this well. He was a deep realist regarding how far he could go toward abolishing the slave trade without simultaneously seeking reforms in the manners and morals of the British people. In other words, national character merely reflected individual character. Public policy and personal policy were inseparable.

Much of the significant policy change in the twentieth century has been achieved by societal movements that gave equal priority to changing hearts and minds as to changing laws. The civil rights movement forced Americans to change their thoughts about racial minorities. The sexual revolution caused Americans to relax their thinking regarding the rules of sexual conduct. The anti-war movement caused many Americans to reconsider their attitudes about military action. Today's burgeoning environmentalist movement is challenging Americans' fundamental attitudes about the environment. Feminism, perhaps the twentieth century's most successful social movement, has changed how society thinks about gender and how women themselves define self-fulfillment. All of these movements have produced policy changes in one form or another, but far more importantly, they have changed how Americans think and what they value. The movements have changed society; they have affected American culture.

SHIFTING DEMOGRAPHICS AND SOFTENING DOGMA

That the issue of culture is so confusing to many only illustrates the problem of a politicized society: we spend far too little time talking about it as Americans. This will have to change, for America's crisis is, at root, a cultural crisis.

The flashpoints of America's cultural politics only illustrate the depth of confusion and disagreement over the basic ideals and values by which we order our lives. Although many Americans share the concerns voiced by political conservatives about declining values, they are reaching the conclusion that many people in politics, including activists, exploit issues for their own purposes, not society's good.

Today the cultural Right must share status with suburban moderates and fiscal conservatives. Both of these groups show concern for values, but are far more libertarian on the social conservative's legislative agenda. The improper framing of cultural issues can backfire quickly, driving critical swing votes into a growing number of other coalitions. For the foreseeable future, appeals that are aimed at traditionalists but are not palatable to suburbanites and baby boomers will be risky.

Traditional-values groups may have seriously misjudged their own constituency. Those who still believe in a moral majority should examine polls that paint an unflattering picture of the core beliefs, even among those to whom they direct their appeals. Many Americans, even the religiously faithful, have softened their orthodox views.

Public-opinion research points to a deepening paradox in society: the combination of commitment to religion with a deepening moral relativism. For example, while 91 percent of the American people consider religion very important in their lives, 63 percent reject the concept of absolutes.[3]

Activist groups and their political allies who run on the basis of a high degree of expected conformity and purity will themselves be forced to come to grips with generational change and a deepening relativism. They will need to move beyond narrowly focused ideological politics to find common ground with the majority, who lack fully formed beliefs. Projects aimed at moral restoration will have to be guided by an appreciation of the impulse toward "tolerance" in America, particularly if the choice appears to be between secular values and religious authority asserting itself in the political arena.

DENATIONALIZING POLITICS

Much of the divisiveness of cultural politics is created by the dominance of groups and leaders who operate at the top of the system, far removed from the neighborhoods where these conflicts are actually worked out. The politics of ideological groups and the welfare of the general public are becoming increasingly incompatible. National political organizations that owe their existence to a narrow core constituency increasingly become marginalized because they reflect a mindset that fewer and fewer Americas share. Ideology simply no longer explains or shapes reality, and no longer inspires a following. We are moving into a future in which national politics and the national government are less relevant to the things people care about most: expanding opportunity, schools that work, safe streets, a less vulgar culture, and renewed community life.

Political power, just as in society and the economy, must move away from the center. Citizens must take back control of issues and debates, particularly those at the local level. Politics will therefore have to be driven from the bottom up. The primary goal of national politicians and movements must be to develop and project a credible vision for all Americans: one that builds social cohesion around the highest ideals even as the pressure toward fragmentation increases. Political leadership in the nineties must summon forth solutions from the people, not just those representing the people under the capitol dome.

Political parties, to remain relevant, will have to find the right balance between specificity of purpose and generality of program. What is needed is classic old-fashioned statesmanship that articulates core American values in the midst of demographic and ideological diversity. The most important objective is to build a new paradigm for debating values that finds a place for the vast majority of Americans who fall between secularism and moralism.

Politics will always be a key platform for debate, including important debates over cultural values. But the culture wars will not be won through moral hectoring, sanctimony, or a politics that places partisanship above social partnership. Cultural conflict is, after all, about culture—the attitudes, values, and habits of a people—which can be reached only minimally through politics. What is needed is persuasion, not imposition.

This is not a call for an exit from politics. Instead it is a call for a new framework that boldly establishes the importance— as well as the limitations—of public policy. This new framework must convey credibly what Americans must do together to create the good society. And it must find a place for the growing number of Americans who believe that cultural strategies are needed to address cultural problems. Linking politics to positive cultural change makes politics more effective and credible, and its accomplishments more long-lasting.

4

LESSONS FROM HISTORY

CULTURAL CHANGE IS NOT LIKELY to occur without spiritual restoration. If the spiritual foundations of the American experiment are to be rebuilt, religion must not only be given its legitimate place once more as a force in society, but also reintegrated with public life in a fashion that is sensitive to religious pluralism and democratic traditions.

When faith is recklessly confused with ideologies and partisan politics, it risks becoming just another "ism"—not a timeless source of transcendent meaning that shapes souls and fortifies civil society. A church known mainly for its political militance is a church that is losing its real power and integrity; this church helps to create—not heal—the wounds of a divided nation.

The issues that are mobilizing the cultural Right are deeply important in themselves, but must be seen as symptoms of a deeper rot, which is more likely to destroy the foundations of a free society than the symptoms themselves. Renewing America's moral values at a foundational level will require far more than simply suppressing symptoms. It will require a deep commitment to the whole of society, rather than the asserting of power through the electoral process. Few of the pressing moral and social problems that are producing anxiety among Americans—whether it be abortion, illegitimacy, urban decay, crime, or the role of homosexuals—are likely to be solved through legislative strategies alone.

The social Right's emergence as a potent force in the political arena has multiple explanations. Some social conservatives have a genuine desire to improve and restore American society; they seek to join in common cause with other concerned Americans. Others want simply to gain back lost power and status for a religious constituency whose monopoly position status in society has been steadily eroded.

There is no denying that the religious Right is engaged in what Richard John Neuhaus describes as a legitimate exercise of the "defensive offense."[1] Religious conservatives believe that a cultural elite and its allies in government have declared war on religion in society. They point to secularist forces that drove prayer and the Ten Commandments out of schools. They also point to the secularists who have sought to squeeze religious beliefs and values into an airtight compartment of private experience.

Thus the sometimes frenzied reaction of social conservatives is often merely a response to the religious and political Left. But religious conservatives only play into the hands of their adversaries with this response. When wedded to political power, religious zeal tends to arouse ancient phobias, leading to the even deeper marginalization of religious activists.

Neuhaus has argued that the public square has been emptied of religious beliefs and values, and thus is left "naked." But this is not entirely the fault of anti-religious forces, as many conservatives are eager to claim. Religious conservatives helped create this condition because they articulated no public philosophy, developed no broadly defined social ethic, and put forward no public arguments that included joint endeavors with unbelievers. As Neuhaus concludes, "By separating public argument from private belief, by building a wall of strict separationism between faith and reason, fundamentalist religion ratifies and reinforces the conclusions of militant secularism."[2]

If the Christian faith becomes just another organized interest group—determined to take over political parties and drive through its own narrowly defined legislative agenda—neither its political power nor its spiritual influence in the culture will grow. If, however, religious conservatives are committed to a holistic social and moral vision for America—one that offers real solutions to the lack of honesty and integrity in politics, seeks to serve the common good of all humankind by offering sound ideas across a spectrum of concerns, and promotes practical ideas for strengthening homes, rebuilding schools, and restoring neighborhoods—then it could offer the leadership a society needs and wants.

But no amount of rethinking will be of significant effect as long as the current confusion continues over the realms of politics, civil society, and religion. Politics does not serve a redemptive function. To imply that it does makes the redemption of individuals and effective politics exceedingly more difficult. Practitioners of religious politics should realize that "Christian" political crusades could drive people from both their faith and their politics.

History's Lessons

Lacking in the current debate over religion and politics is a meaningful historical perspective on the nature of religion's influence in America over several centuries. The very suggestion by secularists, on the one hand, that religion and politics do not mix is contradicted by the very history they helped write. On the other hand, the religious believers who frequently point to the relationship between politics and religion rarely bother to examine exactly how religion and politics have interacted throughout American history.

This brief section is not the place to examine the role of religion in America's history comprehensively. But even a brief examination reveals a basic and inescapable reality: As America has evolved into a more heterogeneous society, the character and role of religion was forced to change along with the country.

The Puritans: All of Life to the Glory of God

During early America, Protestantism's power in shaping public life was undeniably strong. But its public consequences were only an outward expression of its power in shaping the private lives of citizens. No institution, in fact, played a more prominent part in shaping the culture than the church.

Religion had little difficulty shaping politics in colonial America because it exercised power at a fundamental level of culture: the realm of ideas. Puritan Americans had a integrated view of life that is hard to find in today's Christian subculture, which seeks public influence but is more anti-intellectual than perhaps at any time in history. The early Puritans were, in J. I. Packer's words, mostly "conscientious and cultured citizens" who were just as likely to celebrate life as they were to retreat grimly from its joys. The term "Puritan" itself is deeply misleading. Rather than suggesting prudish intolerance of the unchurched, the English Puritans wanted to internally "purify" the Anglican church, whose many blemishes stubbornly defied the Reformation's attempt at ecclesiastical housecleaning.

Unlike much of today's evangelicalism, the Puritans achieved towering accomplishments in many fields and left few aspects of life unexamined. They probably wrote more scholarly books than any similar group of their size in history. Producing great poetry, literature, or scholarship was not inconsistent with their spiritual mission; it was, in fact, a conscious expression of it. The churches, historian Sydney Ahlstrom said, "laid the foundations of the educational system, and stimulated most of the creative intellectual endeavors, by nurturing the authors of most of the books and faculties of most of the schools. The churches offered the best opportunities for architectural expression and inspired the most creative productions in poetry, philosophy, music, and history."[3]

All of life was spiritual for the Puritans. Life was "a seamless fabric integrating heart, soul, body, and mind" in an effort to live all of life for the glory of God.[4] The Puritans had a keen sense of the delicate balances in life because their hearts and minds were deeply engaged in all aspects of life and society. Puritan scholar Leland Ryken describes the study of Puritanism as a discovery of what it means to maintain a paradoxical balance between poles of thought. Puritan doctrine, according to Ryken, was "a vast equilibrium of potential opposites held in harmonious tension." Some examples of this balance include "faith and reason, intellect and feeling, law and grace, the contemplative and active lives, this world and the eternal world, theory and practice, optimism and pessimism."[5]

Central to the Puritan philosophy of life and society was the notion of divine calling. Through this sense of calling they viewed all activity in all spheres of life as an act of worship. This set the Puritans apart from other traditions—including Catholicism, which then saw withdrawal from society as conducive to saintly living. Basic to this sense of calling was a commitment to public duty, only one aspect of which was politics. The cause of constructing a virtuous society by doing good deeds through voluntary means more characterized the Puritan notion of building a holy commonwealth than did mounting political campaigns.

A well-ordered society consisted of social contracts among individuals, and between individuals and the state. The church modeled the best communitarian and individualist ideals, simultaneously building a sense of social solidarity around a shared duty to one another while also acknowledging the "priesthood," and hence inherent worth and dignity, of each individual. Pursuing community and honoring the uniqueness of the individuals were not exclusive goals—they were contiguous. The deep respect for individuals, without regard to class or ecclesiastical status, formed a lasting bond between American democracy and its early Puritanism.

By contrast, today's more experiential descendants of America's early Protestantism apply faith to but a small portion of their lives, and even less so to public life. If they have a public faith at all, it is known mostly for its quest for political power. This truncated faith has boundary lines between sacred and secular, with little cultivation of the commonwealth. This faith has not bothered to translate truth into social ethics, political philosophy, or practical judgment. And unlike that of the early

Protestants, it gives an inordinate attention to the state, while being culturally impoverished.

Religion's Influence Through Revivals

By the time of the Revolutionary War, America's spiritual vision had lost much of its distinctly biblical content and was increasingly fused with other, more secular visions. But still the American sense of destiny, defined largely in terms of divine mission, remained deeply imbedded in its citizens. In an early concession to America's rapid pluralization, religious millennialism evolved into what historian Nathan Hatch has called "civil millenialism"—the belief of the coming ideal society. Thus religion, even in its more secularized form, continued to define America's notion of destiny. The notion of America being a "city on a hill" still strikes a chord today.

Religion has wielded a direct and powerful influence over major events in American history, particularly the episodic outbreaks of religious revival. The struggle for American independence, for example, drew significant strength from eighteenth-century spiritual awakenings. Protestant faith also shaped the constitutional framework and formed many of our ideas of law. Most importantly, it provided the deep and rich subsoil that has nourished the values and habits of a democratic people. Deists and theists alike praised the role of religion in providing for a well-regulated moral life. Deist Thomas Jefferson spoke of the need for being "enlightened by a benign religion, professed, indeed, and practiced in various forms, yet all of them inculcating honesty, truth, temperance, gratitude, and the love of man."

A hundred years after the last revolutionary gun blasted, Protestant revivalists produced the ammunition—moral and material—that would fire fresh shots in another dreadful war. This war was to eradicate what has been regarded as America's original sin: slavery. It is hard to imagine American abolitionism without the fervent faith of Protestants, Quakers, and other believers. One hundred years after the civil war, religious liberalism infused the civil rights and anti-war movements with moral vision and authority. Throughout American history, religion has been a shaping force in society.

Today's Religious Conservatives: Isolation from Culture-Shaping Institutions

Unlike the Puritan forebears, who were deeply engaged in the broader culture, twentieth-century Protestant conservatives have spent the better part of this century withdrawing from the institutions of culture. After the onslaught of theological liberalism and public repudiation in the Scopes trial and other challenges, conservative Protestants sought escape in a world of pronounced isolation. And in isolation they would remain until being provoked out of it some decades later.

It is less the case that cultural power was taken from religious conservatives than they simply relinquished it as they withdrew to a life of separatism and pietism. This faith community enjoys huge commercial and organizational success today, but mostly within the tightly drawn boundaries of its own institutions and channels of communication. Recent attempts at reengagement with the world have been accompanied by the peculiar trappings of conservative Protestantism's own insularity.

After decades of high-profile, sometimes rancorous work, there is little evidence of significant penetration of cultural territory outside of this parochial enclave of separatist Protestantism. Religious conservatives, unlike their liberal counterparts, are conspicuously absent in such disciplines as the arts and humanities; they are rarely found occupying positions of influence in the centers of cultural power that they regularly excoriate, such as journalism, the social sciences, and public policy professions. Consequently, Americans are rarely presented with an intelligent discussion of the faith that was the lodestar of so many of America's founders. It is hard to imagine how political preeminence and lasting accomplishments in public policy can be possible for a group that rarely possesses even token representation in culture-shaping institutions.

The cost of this isolation can hardly be overstated. Had political engagement been accompanied by decades of cultural engagement, the presence of conservative Protestants in politics might not have produced so much acrimony. Social conservatives have tried to regain through politics a cultural hegemony that has long been yielded to others, often by means that appear imprudent and impatient. Fighting cultural wars on political battlegrounds is deeply paradoxical—many of the issues over which the war is declared operate within the cultural realm and lie beyond the law to affect. The suggestion that good law makes good people is more akin to Jean-Jacques Rousseau than to the Scriptures, the charter document of Christian faith.

Compounding the isolation and inexperience is a theological impoverishment that produces factionalism and hairsplitting. Many matters that should be left to practical judgment are often presented in absolutist terms. This mentality provides poor preparation for the practical world of political compromise in which advancement comes, if at all, through small increments.

The impulse toward political absolutism is perhaps the chief source of tension in the traditionalist coalition today. Confusing the infallibility of Scripture with the fallible and often carnal world of practical politics produces the impression that there is little room for reasonable discussion and compromise. Absolutists irresponsibly invoke divine authority on every issue, wrongly suggesting that their faith yields up automatic and specific answers to all political, social, and economic questions.

Civil government may have drawn its foundational authority from higher law, but it draws its day-to-day authority from a different source: the consent of the governed. Political scientist Dean Curry has said that Christians do an injustice to the Scripture when they use it as a "political manifesto." The Bible, he says, is not a "political science textbook."[6] Abraham Lincoln did not quote Scripture to sanction his conduct and policies because he believed that to claim to know God's will produces the sin of pride. Perhaps most damaging to its own success, absolutism chokes out badly needed self-evaluation, and often destroys the generosity that should accompany action toward others.

The greatest concern, therefore, should be for the gospel itself. The Christian faith, after all, is not primarily a cause, an ideology, or a set of morals—although it shapes all of those things. There is a real possibility that the church could be reduced to just another special-interest group in American society, clamoring for political power and hungry for governmental solutions. The words of Samuel Johnson serve as an appropriate reminder: "How small of all that human hearts endure, that part which laws or kings cause or can cure."[7]

This simple realization has guided the actions of believers throughout the ages. Much of the recent organizing by religious conservatives does not fit neatly within an existing American tradition; it represents a new and different one, which many people have found unsettling. The linkages between faith, philosophy, and politics must be restored, but this will not likely be done through a political movement that politicizes religion and religionizes politics.

We now turn to the current relationship between religion and politics, specifically focusing on those who would remove religion from public life in their quest to order society through human reason alone.

5

THE SECULAR HERESY

THE DEBATE ABOUT RELIGION in America has followed a one-dimensional track between two opposing poles, proponents of which sociologist Os Guinness has described as "the reimposers" and "the removers."[1] The reimposers seek to turn the clock back and reestablish a faith-based vision of society that would apply to everyone regardless of individual beliefs; the removers seek to cleanse faith from public life altogether. One would apply private religious views in ways that are hostile to democratic pluralism; the other would rest society on the foundation of secular philosophy in a way that distorts and defies the spirit of American democracy. One would use religious means for religious ends; the other would use secular means for secular ends. Each unwittingly denies America a common basis of public discourse.

Guinness hopes for a new American renaissance that introduces Americans once again to a public philosophy that advances the ideals and interests which are, in large measure, still held in common by Americans. This public philosophy would include a commitment to a new civil public discourse and the pursuit of justice for people of all faiths as well as no faith.

A genuinely American public philosophy would attempt to advance a shared vision for the common good, producing a truce of sorts between the reimposers and removers. An open framework of debate would replace the existing closed systems described by author Arianna Huffington as "coerced traditionalism" of the social Right, on the one hand, or "coerced utopianism" of the secular Left on the other. Both are unrealistic, arbitrary, and incompatible with the American tradition.

Today's reimposers seem to be reassessing the validity of their position, but there is little evidence of similar self-examination among the removers, even as secular belief loses its grip on the general public. The removers can easily recite the few examples in history in which religion was abused, but quite often turn a blind eye to the positive role it has played in securing a healthy, well-ordered society.

Building public discourse around a vision of the common good will be difficult without a common understanding of the essential role that religion and civic morality rooted in religious faith serve in preserving a free society. T. S. Eliot maintained that the development of a culture and religion in a society cannot be isolated from each other. In fact, culture stands on the foundation of religious belief: "We may go further and ask whether what we call the culture, and what we call the religion of a people, are not different aspects of the same thing: the culture being, essentially, the incarnation of the religion of a people."[2]

Because culture is rooted predominantly in religious faith, religious believers should direct their energy and moral vision to shaping the culture. But to do so, religion must be granted entry as a welcome force in affecting civic life. When society is severed from its foundation in religious faith, it will search for alternative sources of ideals and basic beliefs.

Just what remains when a nation's cultural institutions, economics, education, and law are severed from transcendent values? What are the consequences? And what are the alternative sources of moral authority?

THE CULTURE OF NIHILISM

Dangerous things happen when humans substitute self-divinization for God. Friedrich Nietzsche, writing in the spring of 1888, described what he believed would be the history of Western civilization in the coming centuries. In his book *The Will to Power* he sketched the advent of nihilism, which he saw as an unavoidable catastrophe of disorder in society resulting from "the death of God." Nietzsche was not predicting God's actual death. Instead he was suggesting that when God is dethroned and humans become enthralled by their own designs, the divine becomes so irrelevant that he might as well be counted nonexistent.

Nietzsche spoke of a "tortured tension" that would grow decade by decade, "restlessly, violently, headlong, like a river that wants to reach an end."[3] The cause of this coming catastrophe was a temper of life that replaces reflection with "unreflective spontaneity" and calculation. It would grow, Nietzsche predicted, into an unfettered attempt to destroy the past in order to take full control of the present and the future.

This is nihilism, which is opposed to all forms of order based on traditional beliefs and values. And it is the unavoidable end result of the conceit of modernity. The modernist zeitgeist is rooted in the widespread conviction that moral, social, and political order can be manufactured entirely by humans. The result is a society without social order, which Nietzsche predicted would destroy itself.

Personal and social order are some of the most basic needs of humankind. In fact, it is the first need of both the soul and the commonwealth, according to Russell Kirk, with "the inner order of the soul and the outer order of society" intimately linked. "If our souls are disordered, we fall into abnormality, unable to control our impulses. If our commonwealth is disordered, we fall into anarchy."[4]

It is easy to be distracted by today's volcanic debates over single issues and to conclude that if only the antagonists could resolve their differences, society would return to a state of quiet normality. But the great policy disputes reflect a deeper conflict over whether a free society rests upon secular or spiritual foundations.

Eric Voegelin made this point in his discussion of the great line of demarcation in modern politics. It is not a division of liberals (in the classical sense) on one side and statists or totalitarians on the other. Instead, "on one side of that line are all those men and women who fancy that the temporal order is the only order, and that material needs are the only needs, and that they may do as they like with the human patrimony. On the other side of that line are all those people who recognize an enduring moral order in the universe."[5]

THE DOGMA OF RELATIVISM

Secularism has largely supplanted traditional Western morality. Although once only a minority worldview, it has grown dominant by its disproportionate influence in the idea centers of society, such as academia, the media, the entertainment and art communities, and the think tanks. Thus it is not likely that populist campaigns could set in place an alternative belief system. Secularism will only be replaced when compelling alternative frameworks of belief take root within these idea centers of society.

What is entailed in this secular philosophy? One surprising feature is that secularism possesses and propagates its own rigid system of dogma. Allan Bloom, for instance, has referred to those who believe that no reality exists outside of human beings and matter as subscribing to a "dogma of relativism."

Others have characterized the pervasive philosophical materialism of our time as a "secular fundamentalism." Secular true believers, much like their religious counterparts, possess a moral rectitude that is uncommon in an age of declining beliefs. Secularism's adherents hold an unshakable confidence not only in the superiority of their values, but to their right to assert them over others through the institutions of society.

Most secularists are likely to scoff at the idea that they adhere to a dogmatic belief system. Indeed, many see themselves as the dispassionate protectors of society from a surging sectarianism. As Huffington has said, these "proud pragmatists" would deny that this is an ideology at all. They have convinced themselves "that they deal only in rationality, efficiency and progress and that they speak only the mental language of statistics uncontaminated by anything as mystical as 'world view.' "[6]

But it is precisely this worldview that has come to occupy a dominant position in many of America's value-shaping institutions, particularly the social sciences and policy professions. Central to this belief system is the assumption—the conceit—that progress is the inevitable and irreversible result of technological materialism and that the scientific expertise of secularists has surpassed the accumulated cultural heritage of Western civilization in importance.

At the core of this utopian vision is the dream of the manageability of human life and progress through the state—the very dream that has produced the greatest nightmares of the twentieth century in other parts of the world. Nevertheless, it still stirs the prophets and high priests of secular materialism. Secular materialism's utopianist illusion is that "through politics and government action, through the right policies of regulation, control, allocation and provision, society will be made rational and just."[7] In other words, the belief is that the application of human reason through the structures of modern politics will now initiate the reforms that have evaded societies throughout the centuries.

This illusion results in the greatest modern secular heresy—the widely held belief "that the trees move the wind," that material circumstances create spiritual reality.[8] This heresy attempts to substitute economic prosperity, technological prowess and progress, and modern programs and reforms for spiritual truth. The result is a clamor for government solutions, the search for technical gratification, and the elevation of human desires and longings into inalienable rights.

Thus human happiness, or the lack thereof, is defined in terms of politics and law. Human unhappiness is assumed to be caused by some injustice, missing expert analysis, or properly designed program. Government ceases to be seen as a threat to human freedom and progress and instead becomes the primary agent of human happiness. This only reinforces the demand for messianic political movements.

Eventually, of course, politicians find themselves incapable of satisfying the expectations of the body politic. The result, says historian Edward Norman, is "that nasty beast: frustrated hope." After repeated disappointments the electorate inevitably discovers that they have been led to expect too much of governmental action, and that most of the important problems of human life—a happy family life, release from sorrow, freedom from illness, spiritual consciousness, and stable relationships—are "not amenable to political solutions."[9]

THE CULTURAL CONSEQUENCES

Americans have entered a period characterized by frustrated hope. This gnawing reality in American life is producing an unprecedented search for meaning and an escape from a soul-starving secularism. When economic, scientific, and political truths replace religious truths, our spiritual existence slowly ebbs away and the culture atrophies.

Although our greatest need is for an inner ordering of the soul and an outward ordering of individual morality, modern secular liberals are reticent to discuss character and cultural values. The very mention of individual morality implies that individuals, not impersonal forces of history or social structures, are to blame for society's conditions.

Thus liberals, who once were the guardians of the good society, now only talk about dollars and statistical data. This reductionist tendency to shrink humans to simple questions of appropriations is not unlike the conservative search for human renaissance in the form of incentivist magic. The condition of human beings and culture is not understood as a reflection of the human spirit—greatness rooted in goodness, as Tocqueville called it—but by technical and material factors and forces.

This process of subjecting all human experience to the tools of scientific analysis and management can be spiritually impoverishing. It produces a desacrilized world of cold intellectualism. British philosopher Roger Scruton describes this world as one with no lasting common human experience, except "the cold skeletal paradigms that haunt the brains of intellectuals."

What happens to the society that has been severed from its original underpinnings, in which faith, culture, and politics have become fragmented and devoid of meaning and citizens have lost a shared basis for a common life together? The result is loss of community, a declining social order, the erosion of trust in authority, and the increased assertion of human passion through power rather than reasoned argument.

All Americans have much at stake. As Peter Berger has said, when relativism reaches a certain intensity, "absolutism becomes very attractive again." Relativism liberates, but the resulting liberty can produce painful impermanence and uncertainty. People then "seek liberation from relativism."[10]

Alasdair MacIntyre has argued that a rational basis of morality has proven to be impossible again and again. With this evidence mounting, it is time to search for societal foundations that are larger than human beings themselves. If society is severed from these foundations, several negative consequences will follow. It is to these that we next turn.

6

SECULARISM UNLEASHED

WHEN SOCIETY IS SEVERED from its foundations in religious faith, it will search in vain for an alternative source of basic beliefs and ideals. The unleashing of one alternative belief, secularism, reduces law to an extreme rights-based individualism, turns economics into unrestrained, self-serving consumerism, and forces education to forfeit its responsibility to promote the highest ideals of democracy.

THE MODERNIST IMPASSE

By denying a basis for reality outside of the material, cultural nihilism deprives legal systems a connection to a higher law, except for generalizations about the universal rights of humans. Those who fight for a secularized society have their own notion of freedom and legal rights. They do not hold to a concept of traditional liberty, but rather to the libertine concept of freedom without restraints or responsibilities. This vision of social progress is achieved by escaping, not acknowledging, basic human limitations.

The twentieth century has supplied ample evidence that authoritarian tyranny can result just as easily from political movements motivated by this secularist utopianism as from religious or ethnic strife. Without transcendence, morality becomes contingent on human choice. When any concept of a higher law

56

or any notion of self-evident truths has been destroyed, the only real basis for asserting the inestimable moral worth of all of human life is also extinguished. Rationalist humanism, by trying to establish a basis for individual rights without regard for transcendence, defines the human person arbitrarily. The state becomes the only god.

The result is what Phillip Johnson calls "the modernist impasse." This impasse is reached when people conclude that because God is dead they will therefore decide all of the big questions themselves. People are ultimately subjected to "the whims of whoever controls the law-making apparatus."[1] With God out of the picture, "every human becomes a 'godlet'—with as much authority to set standards as any other godlet or combination of godlets."[2]

When government has been made the ally of an extreme rights-based individualism, devoid of a higher morality, it is forced to search for liberation from constraints. But because individual liberties are no longer rooted in a power that transcends the state, individuals are left with only the state or majority rule—not an authoritative evaluator—for protection. Individual rights become vulnerable even as people attempt to strengthen and expand them.

Majority rule is hardly a sufficient basis for protecting the fundamental liberties that may be popular one day and rejected the next. Without a higher basis for judging good and evil, right and wrong, the ends of human action are judged on purely utilitarian grounds—the best for the most. Thus the search for human freedom through legal means can quickly impose a new and unexpected set of constraints on freedom.

This restless search for human progress through legal reforms is the very root of the politicized society. When only the law and politics arbitrate human affairs, everything becomes political—even the most basic human relations. What follows is a state that expands radically even as its competence and legitimacy ebbs. The law degenerates into an arbitrary tool of the politically organized. A right conferred on one group becomes an obligation imposed on another. One person's gain is another's loss. The legal system is forced to find ever more perfect balances and boundaries between conflicting parties and claims.

People expect the law simultaneously to confer the right to sexual freedom as well as freedom from sexual assault; to guarantee gender and racial advantage for some and the protection against reverse discrimination for others; to protect the rights of criminal offenders and the rights of the offended; to guard the rights of free speech but initiate new rights against the insult of hateful speech; to defend both the rights of individuals and communities, and so on. The law has always been expected to strike careful balances in these areas, but never before has it been called on to split conflicting demands with such exasperating precision.

This degree of legal harmony and balance is, of course, beyond the capacity of the law and state agencies to achieve. The law begins to resemble a harried referee who has the impossible task of policing a sport that is both choked by rules and overwhelmed by rule infractions. The pursuit of a just society is reduced to fighting over the rules.

Political philosophers dating back to Aristotle have insisted that republics must renew themselves by returning to first principles again and again. In the case of the law in the late twentieth century, Americans must escape the modernist impasse by rediscovering the basic assumptions about human beings, society, and the law that originally shaped the American republic. This begins with the recognition that a continuation of secularist assaults on the transcendent foundations of law could turn the Declaration of Independence, the U.S. Constitution, and the Bill of Rights into worthless pieces of paper.

CAPITALISM'S CULTURAL CONTRADICTIONS

If there is no reality beyond the material, then nothing exists *except* the material. This means that in the vast arena of economics the highest purposes are production and consumption.

People not only live for bread alone; they live only to pursue it in ever greater quantities, often with little regard for the means of acquiring it. Quality in life is measured in terms of quantities.

America's common moral heritage and language have been subjugated to the cant and calculation of self-interest. Moral ethicists and theologians, once welcome voices in public life, now occupy a small section of the bleachers far removed from the economic playing field. Their concerns and language now seem alien and off-putting to the utilitarian-minded modernist.

Instead, the language of economics, such as jobs, programs, incentives, and capital formation, is the language that makes the modern rationalist comfortable—whether the rationalist is a government-minded Democrat or a business-minded Republican. They are comfortable with economics because they see it as impersonal, quantifiable, and subject to expert study and calculation.

Attempts to surround human economic activity with spiritual meaning and transcendent claims have been abandoned by most in the Western world. The chief feature of the twentieth century has been the pursuit of economic progress through technical and material means. William Van Dusen Wishard, for example, describes the creation of "the economic man" as the basic objective of the human community in the twentieth century. "We have differed on how best to reach that goal, but whether it was capitalism, Marxism or Socialism, creating Economic Man was the ultimate aim."[3]

For much of the twentieth century, the philosophical foundation of Western society has been secular materialism, which translates into economic determinism in one form or another. If spiritual truth and mystery have no place in the universe, economic factors not only explain reality, they are believed to shape it. In other words, get the economics right and the human spirit will flourish and civilization will soar. The good society is assumed to be a creation entirely of economics.

A critical theme in American political philosophy dating back to its founding has been the question of whether the republic could be preserved through self-interest alone or whether its survival depended on the cultivation of virtue. Many have believed virtue to be an essential source of strength for a republic.

The Federalist Papers reveal the founders' basic assumptions about human nature: they believed in the corruptibility of human beings. The debate was not over whether people's propensity for self-interest existed; it was about whether society should view it benignly. Was the individual pursuit of private interests—primarily a driving search for riches—an adequate foundation for a well-ordered society?

Some framers, such as Thomas Jefferson, believed the common good would be served by simply unleashing and harnessing the pursuit of interests. They thought that unfettered exchange among free men and women would produce happy and prosperous individuals, resulting in social harmony. The search for greater economic prosperity was the very definition of the pursuit of happiness.

Yet other founders concerned themselves with a specter that had haunted political theorists long before America's founding: that selfish propensities, if not accompanied by religious and moral discipline, would corrode commerce and corrupt republics. George Washington did not think a free republic could be maintained without a virtuous people. James Madison saw the need for passions to be controlled and reformed. The polity, they believed, required the nourishment that character provides. In fact, limited government rested upon these virtues of self-government. Economic freedom without ethical vitality is impossible.

Historically, faith has tempered the narrow pursuit of self-interest. While commercialism has encouraged self-interest, religion has cultivated character by reminding people both of the sin of sloth and the sin of slavishly pursuing wealth. Faith has provided a needed balance between the pursuit of private interest and the common good.

But America's economic debate now lacks that vital linkage, for it focuses more on taxes and trade than on transcendence. Partisan debates follow a predictable path: how much to spend and on what; who to tax and by how much. Whether it is programs or profits, the debate rarely reaches the higher plane of personal or national purpose.

Commerce without a moral compass can easily degenerate into a scramble for wealth that has little regard for honest work, industry, thrift, and deferral of gratification. Tocqueville, as observed elsewhere, was deeply concerned about a pernicious materialism that would substitute wealth for work, creating a commercial culture that would subvert the very virtues on which it depends.

Twentieth-century Americans have separated economics from the ethical foundations that should guide all human inter-course. The pursuit of wealth has become mostly an end in itself, rather than a means to the realization of higher ends, including a virtuous life with strong communities and families.

Economics is rooted in the culture, and thus reflects the beliefs and meaning systems that are embodied in the culture. In other words, the commercial world mirrors what Americans value. The nation's economic life will reflect whether a culture values individual consumption, amusement, and impulse grati-fication or duty, honor, and integrity in relationships toward fam-ily and community.

Much like the rights-based individualism that drives the legal system, economics reflects a philosophy of life that empow-ers individuals without giving them a capacity for unselfish devo-tion to the common good. Political scientist Mark Henrie describes the rights-based politics of the liberal state and mar-ket individualism as "the twin homogenizing powers."[4] The neg-ative effects on civil society and such mediating structures as strong families and autonomous communities are the same.

Nonetheless many who promote the family and faith in soci-ety are often the least critical of unlimited economic freedoms. They only see the danger of restricting the economic impulse, not of letting it run rampant. George Will accuses traditionalist politics of being blind to the contradictions of capitalism. Repub-licans, he says, "see no connection between the cultural phenomena they deplore and the capitalist culture they promise to intensify; no connection between the multiplying evidence of self-indulgence and national decadence (such as pornography, promiscuity, abortion, divorce and other forms of undiscipline) and the unsleeping pursuit of ever more immediate, intense and grand material gratifications."[5]

Other traditionalists, such as Russell Kirk, have argued that conservatism cannot be "merely a defense of industrialism and industrial free market economics." Conservatism is about "the cultivation and conservation of certain values, or it is nothing." Conservatives too frequently view markets as the ultimate value and "ultimate arbiter of values." The result is that we have committed "taxidermy on moral categories," draining them "of their richness and stuffing them full of sawdust talk of rights, interests, and interstate commerce."[6]

If economic activity is severed from its transcendent foundations, such as what has occurred in recent decades, society will continue to pay a heavy price in the declining quality of its culture, the corruption of commercial life, and the eventual waning of economic liberties under the weight of a powerful state.

CULTURAL TRANSMISSION OR CULTURAL OMISSION?

No institution of American life has been more affected by the spirit of the age, to more dire effect, than the education system. The very thought of introducing transcendent values into the schools conjures up fears of sectarian religion permeating public education, or as one school superintendent described it, the fear of public schools being converted into parochial schools. America's education system has become the chief battlefield of America's cultural conflicts.

From the founders to the present, much lip service has been paid to society's dependence on education for survival. Educators carry a heavier burden for the preservation of culture than any other elite profession. As philosopher Ronald Nash has pointed out, education forms "the great link in the chain of civilization without which it cannot hold." Teachers are "both the conservators and the transmitters of culture. It is through the transmission of these ideas that future generations come to appreciate the highest ideals of our country and civilization."[7]

Perhaps most important to consider in this discussion of education is the prevalent educational philosophy, and how its basic assumptions affect the health of democratic society.

A traditional view of education would draw from the wisdom of the ages. It would transmit a free society's highest ideals. It would impart the knowledge necessary for democratic participation. And it would recognize, as education has recognized since Aristotle, that the ultimate end of learning is virtue and character. Let this kind of education and training lapse for one generation, H. Richard Niebuhr wrote, "and the whole grand structure of past achievements falls into ruins."[8]

It would seem, then, that education in a democracy would serve to protect the democratic regime by preserving democratic values. Students would be literate in the basics of Western civilization: our economics, system of limited and divided government, and history and unique constitutional heritage.

What is the prevailing philosophy of education? Consider the textbooks, teaching literature, instructional films, school activities, and programs. Human beings are the final authority; there is no transcendent belief. Values, it would seem, are strictly personal matters. Paul Vitz has demonstrated the fact that school textbooks have almost completely excised any reference to America's true religious heritage. He has said that parents are "being taxed to support schools that systematically fail to represent their beliefs, values, history and heritage." They are supporting and subsidizing a system that is "liquidating our most cherished beliefs."[9]

American society will be best served by citizens who know and care about freedom and democracy, and its foundations and requirements. What happens in the schools affects all of us, liberal or conservative; Protestant, Catholic, Jew, or other.

As the evidence of relativism's bankruptcy lies like wreckage all around them, many of education's trendsetters and policy makers simply refuse to yield on the dogma of relativism. In the midst of relativism's obvious failings, many educators continue to loath the notion of truth, ultimate values, or ethical imperatives. Education's main aim was once to forge character and wisdom. In addition to learning the basics, the job of education has been to equip children for adulthood—for work, responsibility, and independent living in a democratic and free society.

How are we preparing the future generations? C. S. Lewis compared old and new approaches to education, answering this question. The old, he said, initiated the young into society, much as grown birds teach their young how to fly. But the new deals with the young "more as the poultry-keeper deals with young birds—making them thus or thus for purposes of which the young birds know nothing. In a word, the old was a kind of propagation—men transmitting manhood to men: the new is merely propaganda."[10] Lewis found a deep relativism at the core of the educational chaos, which viewed values as entirely subjective matters commanding no loyalty.

Without transcendent values, there is no basis for concluding that honesty, lawfulness, or any other basic ingredient of a free society is more than merely a reflection of one person's egoistic wishes, tastes, and preference. What is the locus of authority in such a relativistic system? Is it public opinion, majority rule, or simply each person for himself or herself? There simply is none. Whatever else the failings of American education may be, it is falling woefully short of its obligations to preserve a democratic order.

THE PROPER ROLE OF RELIGION AND POLITICS

AS WE HAVE SEEN in the previous two chapters, secularism has not imparted society with the transcendent foundations it needs. Clearly, religion must neither be eradicated from public life nor forced on nonbelievers. A vision of the good society must include the proper ordering of religion and politics.

A "CHRISTIAN AMERICA"?

Calling for a return to a "Christian America" through politics does not reflect the proper ordering of religion and politics. And it is neither historically accurate nor politically wise in today's multicultural society. America's founders were certainly not "religious rightists," even though many were committed Protestant believers. They converted their worldview into a social and political philosophy and then argued on that level, not on the level of sectarian religion. By so doing, they created a broad basis for securing the values needed to undergird American democracy.

The real legacy of America's Christian forebears was their successful struggle to build a democracy that would be open to immigrants from around the world, regardless of religion or creed. They recognized that religious faith was an indispensable wellspring from which the morality of a free and self-governing people would flow. Although they recognized the divine origins of government, they did not think America's religious identity

65

should be asserted through politics or government. This was the duty of individuals and religious institutions operating freely in society.

Advocates of a "Christian America" are wrong to claim sole proprietorship of America's heritage; rather it resembles a partnership between religious and other philosophical influences. The constitutional fabric was sown as much out of natural law as it was out of supernatural revelation, even though the Scriptures and divine providence supplied vital guidance. Religion's primary power was consistent with a more important purpose: shaping the dominant cultural and moral ideals that served as the foundation of a well-ordered society.

Many people assume that recent forms of religious activism in the political process have been the norm for centuries, only falling out of favor recently. But this is simply not so. They would do well to read Tocqueville's *Democracy in America*, the authoritative analysis of America's social and political life during the nineteenth century. Tocqueville was struck by both religion's force in American society and the proscribed nature of the realm that religion occupied.

Tocqueville, a European who was horrified by the ferocity of the French revolution's attack on religion, found in America "the spirit of religion and the spirit of freedom" both marching in the same direction. He deemed America one of "the freest and most enlightened nations in the world" and saw its people filled with fervor for all the "duties of religion."[1]

To such an outside observer as Tocqueville, religion "retained a greater influence over the souls" of people than any country in the world. Religion's role in the society of the early 1800s was one of nourishing the habits of restraint, industry, and tranquillity that were thought necessary to maintain republican institutions.

Although religion's influence over manners and morals— the "habits of the heart"—was vast, organized religion maintained a studied distance when it came to political parties and public affairs. In America, said Tocqueville, religion "exercises but little influence upon the laws and upon the details of public opinion; but it directs the customs of community, and, by regulating domestic life, it regulates the state."[2]

In other words, its indirect influence was considerable; its direct influence minimal and guarded. The clergy, in particular, were careful to preserve the unique and honored station they occupied in society. Ministers of the gospel "eschewed all parties," filled no public appointments, and were "excluded by public opinion" (and by law in several states) from serving in legislatures.[3]

Tocqueville's recorded observations, now over a hundred fifty years old, serve as a timely reminder of what is at stake for religious belief when boundaries are confused. Tocqueville observed: "The church cannot share the temporal power of the state without being the object of a portion of that animosity which the latter excites."[4] In forming an alliance with a political power, and particularly partisan powers, "religion augments its authority over a few and forfeits the hope of reigning over all." If religion becomes "mixed up with the bitter passions of the world it may be constrained to defend allies whom its interests, and not the principle of love, have given to it; or to repel as antagonists men who are still attached to it, however opposed they may be to the power with which it is allied."[5]

And so the role of religion was seen as higher than that of politics, and thus was to be preserved from the passions and prejudices that power generates. The lesson for today's secularized culture is twofold: restore religion's legitimate role in the realm of culture, and help shape and articulate a vision for the common good in the realm of politics that goes beyond a simplistic moral agenda. A few legislative fixes will not restore health to a society molded by the forces of secularism and modernity.

The real aim of Christians in previous centuries was to create a good society by voluntary means, not just through a political movement in search of "good" legislative policies. This would be a society in which the natural end of humans, as T. S. Eliot said, is virtue and well-being in community, established for the benefit of all. The good society would commit itself as much to the restoration of culture as to the correctness of its politics, understanding that culture more shapes, than is shaped by, politics.

Conversely, it can be said that a society has ceased to be Christian when faith no longer regulates the values of the people, when that society no longer consciously patterns its meaning-defining activities on faith, and when its dominant philosophy and concepts of law and justice are no longer anchored to transcendent reality. Whether or not a nation can be said to be Christian is more a function of the patterns of belief and conduct of its people than the verbal representations of its leaders. To return a nation to its spiritual and theological roots requires much more than winning elections. It requires winning the hearts and minds of citizens and mobilizing leaders across many vital sectors and institutions of society.

Unfortunately, many people trust in power and the state to effect change in the realm of personal and social values. Many see politics as the only platform for addressing the moral failings of America. This is why so very much is expected of politics.

GOVERNMENT'S IMPORTANT, BUT LIMITED, ROLE IN A FREE SOCIETY

In a free society, the state must be a subsidiary of society. The state must be society's servant, not its master. It is equally wrong for either religious believers or secularists to try to master society through the state. The more realistic mission should be to minimize the expansive power and role of the government in society, working to restore the institutions of civil society.

The Catholic doctrine for this rightful ordering of society is called subsidiarity. It was first articulated by Pope Pius XI in 1931 and was recently reformulated by Pope John Paul. Pope John Paul has explained subsidiarity as follows: "A community of a higher order should not interfere in the internal life of a community of a lower order, depriving the latter of its functions, but rather should support it in case of need and help to coordinate its activity with the activities of the rest of society, always with a view to the common good."[6]

This concept reaffirms a basic principle of America's founding political philosophy that the central government should be limited, the state should not encroach on the functions of civil society, and all should strive to preserve civil society. To the extent that we succeed, individuals are then free to regulate their own affairs. To the extent that we fail, government takes on responsibilities for which it has neither competence nor authority.

The government's greatest harm may come less in the form of its annual cost to taxpayers and more in its destructive influence on civil society and its institutions, such as the family, church, neighborhoods, and other mediating structures that provide humankind meaning and life-sustaining support. A society that wishes to remain free and strong will protect these institutions from governmental overextension and politicization.

Restoring these institutions, once weakened, is a daunting task. Government is more capable of disrupting the proper ordering of civil society than it is restoring it once weakened. The temptation to think of governmental remedies for problems in civil society is understandable. But attempts to use state power to restore lost cultural authority and social cohesion—without appreciating politics' limitations—could unwittingly contribute to the further eroding of these vital mediating structures.

Catholic scholar John Courtney Murray attempted to impart an understanding of the different spheres of spiritual and temporal life. The temporal is important, but the spiritual holds primacy over the believer. The work of the spiritual realm is primarily that of ministering to the conscience and souls of people, and by extension the soul and conscience of society. The spheres must work in harmony, but never at the expense of the spiritual. The spiritual realm is neither the servant nor master of the political order; it belongs to a different sphere.[7]

Harmony in society is destroyed either by a radical separation of the state from its necessary grounding in transcendent faith or by the church or the state trespassing on the institutional authority and functions of the other. And when harmony is destroyed, human dignity and freedom are threatened.

Disharmony has been created in America by the state's secularization of life and the marginalization of religious faith in public life. But disharmony can also be created by religious activism that confuses the legitimate and urgent need to restore values with illegitimate attempts to place religious authority over government, and by extension, to the populace. The temptation to reach for power in a politicized society may seem entirely rational. It appears to offer quick and concrete results—one officeholder is replaced by another and the victor substitutes his or her power agenda for that of the vanquished. But these victories can be hollow and are often quickly reversed.

This analysis should not be confused with the argument used by secularists to promote their version of church-state separation. Nor should it be seen as an attempt to suggest that politics is unimportant. Instead it is a call for a new engagement in policy making and culture shaping that is guided by a realistic set of assumptions and a cognizance of both the promise and perils of politics.

ROLE OF THE CHURCH IN A FREE SOCIETY

Those whose loyalty is to the first things of faith should protect the power and integrity of faith over the souls of individuals. In a sincere desire to fulfill their responsibilities, some have politicized their faith. Many Christian Americans have come perilously close to believing that being an active Republican or conservative is an inseparable dimension of practicing their Christian faith.

There are understandable reasons for this, not the least of which is the unfortunate way in which cultural polarization has tracked partisan alliances and faultlines. Nevertheless, although Christian duty calls men and women to participate in policy shaping, they should not confuse it with the kingdom of God.

Christians should not follow the heretical practice of attaching the name of Christ to particular political movements or parties. The church, which exists for the "glory of God and the sanctification of souls" (T. S. Eliot), risks losing its spiritual power and authenticity when it uncritically and unreservedly aligns itself with temporal partisan movements.

"My kingdom is not of this earth," said Jesus. Though the kingdom of God shapes the temporal, nevertheless it is of a different realm—one that reigns within the hearts of those who chose to accept it. To confuse these realms is to confound "the permanent with the transitory, the absolute with the contingent." Eliot even said that the practice of identifying a particular form of government with the Christian faith was "a dangerous error." We must be careful not to identify faith with a form of social organization that is always in a state of change.[8]

Should the church be conservative, liberal, or radical? Should it be unified or divided in its support for a position? Should it be placid and pliable or critical and non-conformist? These questions are worth pondering, for the answers may be less clear than often assumed. When the church identifies itself as conservative, it may be conserving the wrong things; when it is liberal, it may be too approving of reckless innovation; if it becomes revolutionary, it may be undermining the very permanent things that it has set out to preserve.

When people use the Christian faith to endorse a social or political program, they can rightfully expect it to be judged for its failings. This is true whether the issue is party politics, such as during the 1992 presidential campaign, or if it is policies, ideologies, or economics.

Those who have casually assumed that democratic capitalism came to us from Mount Sinai in the form of chiseled stone are often sobered to discover that the Scriptures provide little direct advice on building social systems and little encouragement for those who preoccupy themselves with public policy or economics. Libertarian scholar Doug Bandow, a strong defender of market capitalism on practical and moral grounds, has cautioned against confusing the kingdom of God with a particular social or economic system. "There is no explicit endorsement of any type of economic system, no equation of capitalism or socialism with the kingdom of God." Many such prescriptions applied to Israel in the Old Testament. But this ancient regime, with its special covenant status, is not a good analogue for secular America.[9]

Indeed, it has often been Christians who have rightfully raised concerns about the spiritual sterility of extreme commercialism and have attempted to preserve the link between economic freedom and moral responsibility. Free markets by themselves do not assure a well-ordered and free society; they can even undermine the very virtues that produced prosperity in the first place.

As Tocqueville observed, the American republic could not survive without public-spiritness mixed in with self-interest and ambition. Among the many important functions of religion in society that Tocqueville noted, perhaps religion's chief contribution was countering the acquisitive individualism in American society. In a commercial society, people cannot be cured of the love of riches, but religion can cause them to enrich themselves by none other than honest means, to value the "natural bonds and legitimate pleasures of home," and to discover that "an orderly life is the surest path to happiness."

We should not unreservedly attach a seal of divine authorization to our excessively commercial society or grant it moral superiority without acknowledging that market systems can fuel greed, selfishness, and a host of other distortions and abuses. When religion simplistically and uncritically supplies the moral authority to partisan claims in dozens of social and economic policies that are actually filled with moral ambiguity, religion's capacity to stand above and in judgment over all human activity is significantly weakened.

8

❧

FOUR PERSONAL REQUIREMENTS

MUCH OF THE CONFUSION that has surrounded religion and politics results directly from the intellectual impoverishment of our age. It is a result of too little interest in the role of the historical Judeo-Christian faith of Western civilization. This lack of awareness produces a search for quick fixes for vexing problems and substitutes a religious activism for more effective forms of citizenship rooted in a broader vision for the common good.

Today's challenge, similar to that faced by the founders, is to construct the broadest possible basis for the needed shared values for America's institutions not to fail. These values—values affecting individual conduct, family commitments, and public life—are far too important to be framed in terms that empower and appeal to a single political faction. After all, this debate concerns the values that undergird and guide the society in which we all must live.

What would be the components of this broader framework and more inclusive political appeal? How can faith be integrated more effectively, intelligently, and legitimately in the project of restoring America? These questions deserve examination. In this chapter we will look at four personal requirements for those who seek to integrate their faith with their public life. In chapter nine we will turn to five public responsibilities that are necessary for proper engagement with society.

#1: START WITH CORRECT ASSUMPTIONS ABOUT HUMAN LIFE AND SOCIETY

To restore lost values effectively believers must develop correct assumptions, the chief of which is a healthy realism regarding both the possibilities and perils of politics. They should adopt a view of humanity and the world that not only is consistent with scriptural teaching but with the entire Western tradition. The experience of history suggests that heavily hyped social reforms aimed at rebuilding a moral society through the ballot box, whether liberal or conservative, deserve skepticism.

Social and political progressives have tried to reshape societal institutions, in Tocqueville's words, on "novel, ingenious, original lines." When one experiment is no more successful than the previous one, these engineers of social progress ask to be judged by their good intentions, not by their actual achievements. As Edmund Burke said of the French revolutionaries, "in the manifest failure of their abilities, they take credit for their intentions."[1]

A realistic view of the world provides a rationale for effective action rooted in modest expectations. Reinhold Niebuhr modeled this kind of hopeful but realistic leadership. He maintained that the quest for earthly utopias lead to more suffering, whether the movements are secular or religious. He also maintained that anti-utopianism must not consist of simply avoiding the call to social action and change. He said, "We need prophets who know all about man and yet believe in him, whose faith in his destiny as a son of God has been won without ignorance of his real crimes and sins."[2] A despairing fatalism is just as forbidden as a crusading utopianism.

Realism, therefore, produces constructive engagement. No one is justified in concluding, as some are prone to saying, "there is nothing we can do about it." But neither is there a basis for concluding that with just a little more effort the world can be made happy and sinless. We must plunge into the social and political problems of the world, as Jacques Ellul said, "not in the hope of making it a paradise, but simply in order to make it tolerable."[3]

To make the world more tolerable, believers are called into public life to nurture the values and habits that sustain a humane community. Culture formation is more urgent than policy prescription, even though providing workable solutions for a host of societal problems is certainly a part of forming the culture. In other words, faith's job is to foster the sorts of things that public policy programs rarely achieve.

#2: MEASURE ATTITUDES AND CONDUCT BY TRANSCENDENT CLAIMS

The world must be viewed the way God views it—lost but loved. Therefore all of creation, including humankind, must be treated the way God would treat it. The individual's actions in the social and political arena should never contradict the highest ideals of the faith, such as "loving your neighbor as yourself." The world's methods and techniques are more known for their violation than their veneration of this ethic. But there is a higher way—a way that does not confuse moral means and ends.

In Jesus Christ, Ellul has said, the means and ends are joined. Thus the world ought to be preserved "by God's methods, not by man's technical work."[4] This higher way demands a revolutionary style of life and presence within human history that steadfastly "refuses to cave in to despair" over circumstances.[5] This style of life also stubbornly refuses to resort to desperate means.

If mistakes are made—and in politics they often are—faith should not be implicated as it quite often is. Many times the message delivered in polarizing appeals is designed more to rally the faithful than to convert the unconvinced. When these appeals are inconsistent with the claims of faith not only are they ineffective, they are wrong. The apostle Paul frequently admonished believers to show integrity, seriousness, and the soundness of speech that cannot be condemned, to be kind and gentle, not to slander or be resentful, and to show respect and humility toward all people, including one's enemies. In far too many cases, Christians have taken their cues from either their secular foes or conservative allies, forgetting their unique calling to anchor all of their activity in Christian ethics.

Os Guinness describes an impetuous "whatever it takes" mentality that ignores the inconsistency between ends and means, and thus becomes "less moral than the stated intentions, less successful, less conservative, and less Christian." Guinness adds that the cardinal lesson of social movements in American history is that "high goals require effective strategies, and in the long run effective strategies are also the most principled, the most persuasive, and the most American."[6]

This ethic inspired Martin Luther King to forsake a politics of resentment for a philosophy of nonviolent resistance that was rooted in spiritual power. Only through an inner spiritual transformation, he said, "do we gain the strength to fight vigorously the evils of the world in a humble and loving spirit." When we are not conformed to the world, but transformed with "the gospel glow of the early Christians," we will be saved from "speaking irresponsible words which estrange without reconciling."[7]

This, sadly, is not always the spirit that guides public action. John Seel has said that many American Christians have been "more American than Christian, more dependent on historical myths than spiritual realities, more shaped by the flag than the cross."[8] Some Christian activists are blinded by an idolatrous pursuit of power based on an attitude of "we were here first" and by a majoritarian myth that destroys individuals' love for people with whom they disagree.

Followers of Christ—not their secular foes or political allies—are uniquely constrained by the demands of their faith. Thus there is no room for attitudes or tactics that are inconsistent with their own transcendent claims, such as a joyless and despairing outlook on life. Nor is there justification for methods that appeal to anger, fear, slander, or retaliation, which remain prevalent in many direct-mail solicitations.

Christ's answers to the problem of culture are one thing; "Christian" answers are another. It is deeply painful to subject one's attitudes and prejudices to the gospel, and to ask how much of the accumulated attitudes are simply a product of middle-class American Protestantism. Jesus preached about the kingdom within, which is the only antidote to the ugliness that grows out of the heart of people.

Indifference and inaction will not restore the good society, but neither will the form of action that confuses means and ends and therefore destroys the very transcendence it aims to restore.

#3: LIVE A LIFESTYLE OF REPENTANCE, FORGIVENESS, AND LOVE

Few activities involve a greater risk of producing charges of sanctimony than public moralizing. Moralists can quickly become indifferent to their own carnality and unworthiness, unconsciously slipping into attitudes of self-righteousness and seeing the world as being beyond redemption. Jesus condemned the pharisaical outlook that boasted, "I thank God that I am not like the rest of them." Jesus was not uncomfortable with sinners, nor was he surprised by sin. He came to seek and save those who were lost.

Jesus found that the righteous were more blinded by their moral goodness than sinners were blinded by their sin. Those who seek to modify the morality of the world should remind themselves regularly of their own participation in and culpability for the fallen condition of the world. When fallen individuals repent for their responsibility in the condition of the world, they provide a means to avoid the recriminations and hatreds that too frequently accompany bitter public disputes.

Aleksandr Solzhenitsyn and Fyodor Dostoyevsky, both towering contenders against Russian tyranny, made the struggle for repentance and forgiveness a central theme in their writings. Those who turn from forgiveness to bitterness only mirror the character they so detest in their enemies and have, in fact, become overpowered by them. The root of our problems and the source of our recovery lie within us.

Dostoyevsky believed that bitterness and resentment drive humankind toward the abyss of dehumanization. Those who practice faith and believe it is the very foundation of civil social order have a special obligation to demonstrate the demand of that faith to love their bitterest enemies unconditionally. The power to act in a spirit of forgiveness is a supernatural power that those lacking faith cannot replicate.

We must recognize that our enemies are no less the object of God's love than are we. Abortion, the abuse of women and children, homosexuality, and pornographic addictions are only loathsome reflections of the same sinful condition carried by those who contend against these sins.

Says David Walsh, "Without a pure, disinterested love from the start, we have no way of reaching it in the end; without a self-effacing modesty concerning our goal, we have no way to resist the most excessive self-aggrandizement; and without a firm recognition of the reality of good and evil, we inevitably succumb to the worst temptations of power."[9] Without recognizing the humanity of others, differences are not settled. This only leads to an overpowering of one's opponent through a naked will to power.

To love unconditionally and forgive is not to be confused with tolerance, a term that can imply moral neutrality and consent. The spirit of forgiveness accepts others while rejecting their conduct or convictions. Few terms are more loaded with self-deception and distortion than the contemporary concept of tolerance. The growing calls for Americans to be more tolerant have not produced citizens who act with genuine benevolence toward one another.

Fostering a spirit of forgiveness not only serves a spiritually redemptive influence, but is socially redemptive. Niebuhr and G. K. Chesterton both argued that forgiveness made it possible for opposing groups to fight to the end without denying the other's humanity. This is a particular burden for those who frame the public argument in the claims of private religious faith. Civil society involves the exchange of ideas—even vigorous arguments over competing ideas and values. But to disagree in a civil society, says John Courtney Murray, is "to share enough in common to have something to disagree about."

"The whole premise of the public argument, if it is to be civilized and civilizing, is that consensus is real, that among the people, everything is not in doubt, but that there is a core of agreement, accord, concurrence, acquiescence. We hold certain truths; therefore we can argue about them." Without this sense of acknowledging the other's humanity, debates degenerate into shrill mutterings. Whoever wins, society loses, and "the barbarian is at the gates of the city."[10]

Dietrich Bonhoeffer, who paid with his life for not bowing to Nazi pressure to remain silent in the face of Hitler's atrocities, remained a steadfast disciple of Jesus Christ to the end. He faced the firing squad without hate because he was passionately committed to reflecting the unconditional love of Christ in his life.

Bonhoeffer warned his generation about the irresistible pull toward a self-righteousness that destroys one's capacity to engage in heroic acts of love and mercy. This kind of judgment is "the forbidden objectivization of the other person," the result of which is the destruction of "single-minded love." We are not forbidden to have our own thoughts about other people or their shortcomings, but only to the extent that it offers us "an occasion for forgiveness and unconditional love."[11]

#4: TWO CITIES, TWO LOVES, TWO LOYALTIES

Believers have a special obligation to act upon the convictions of faith, but also to be restrained by the reservations it produces about earthly reforms.

Saint Augustine served as Bishop of Hippo in Northern Africa during the Roman Empire's decline and fall in the fourth century. In his day, the world was polarized much as it is today. National decline for the Romans provoked a bitter debate—a culture war—focusing on who was to blame for the fall. The believers blamed it on the appalling decadence that had encircled them. Roman culture had become obsessed with leisure and sex. Its art and culture, particularly its officially funded and sponsored art, had become highly decadent. Fewer and fewer people worked, and increasing numbers lived off the state. Taxes went through the roof.

In offering his defense against charges that the church did not enthusiastically serve the state, and thus contributed to the state's collapse, Augustine presented an interpretation of events that is relevant today. He said the protagonists on either side of the conflict should be seen as members of two cities that have continuously coexisted, collided, and tried to co-opt each other throughout history. In the "city of God" at least there is the possibility of real peace, justice, and human happiness. In the "city of man" baser values and counterfeit versions of brotherly love and justice exist.

According to Augustine, all of human history and culture may be viewed as the interplay of these two cities. The distinguishing factor, he said, is the object of their love. Otherworldliness produces a passion for tidying up this world; neglect is a form of worldliness. Where there are good Christians, said Augustine, there are good citizens.[12] Similarly, C. S. Lewis maintained that the Christians who "did the most for the present world were precisely those who thought the most of the next."[13]

Christians are in the world but their ties are elsewhere—they serve another master, another order, another claim. Every public enterprise, political organization, and social reform should produce this kind of tension and skepticism, for in every such enterprise there is potential imbalance. As Martin Luther King said, "As Christians we must never surrender our supreme loyalty to any time-bound idea, for at the heart of our universe is a higher reality—God and his Kingdom of love—to which we must be conformed."[14]

9

FIVE PUBLIC RESPONSIBILITIES

BUILDING ON THE FOUR PERSONAL REQUIREMENTS outlined in the previous chapter, we now turn to five needed public responsibilities. An integrated faith will include a proper engagement with society. Through this engagement we will promote the values that are needed to restore the good society.

#1: PRESERVE THE FAITH FROM POLITICIZATION

As Richard John Neuhaus has stated, "The first thing to be said about public life is that public life is *not* the first thing."[1] If the church does not assert custody over the inner life of believers, it cannot hope to assert influence over the outer life of society. The church must preserve itself from politicization to minister healing to hurting and lonely souls.

The church is the servant of a higher order. The church's greatest service, according to historian Christopher Dawson, is "to keep her own inheritance intact and not allow her witness to be obscured by letting herself be used as the instrument of secular power and politics."[2] Dawson continues,

> The idea that the spiritual life of society should be ruled and guided by a political party would have appeared to our ancestors a monstrous absurdity. The spiritual order possessed its own organization, that of the church, which was held to tran-

scend all the rest in importance and which exercised a profound influence on human life from cradle to grave.[3]

There are many who would harness the church in great campaigns of moral rearmament and patriotic causes—often wor-
thy. But as John Courtney Murray has said, the believer must
not "merge his religious and his patriotic faith, or submerge one
into another." Ultimate allegiances will transcend the nation.[4]

#2: PURSUE IDEALS, NOT IDEOLOGIES

Ideological crusades have been used throughout history to try
to remake society along new lines and new religions, such as
when French revolutionaries worked to install a new religion in
the place of the Christian faith. Ideological crusades can also
take the form of religion being forced into the public square,
through such efforts as replacing secularist ideologies with those
of the religious Right.

In his critically acclaimed book *Culture Wars*, James Davison
Hunter refers to a deep division running across America between
traditionalist and progressive alliances. Each side holds a view
of the world that is diametrically opposed to the other; each har-
bors a deep hostility against the other. Hunter says that each
side of the cultural divide judges the other to be ideological
extremists, illegitimate "by virtue of the substance of its message."[5]

When powerful forces align themselves against others'
beliefs, they can be easily drawn into such predictable ideological postures that only serve to purify their resolve against the
"enemy," and little more. Responding in like manner to attacks
is human nature, but such an approach is not effective over time.
And in the case of traditionalists, this response is inconsistent
with their very tenets of belief. When religion reinforces a shal-
low and fragmented public discourse, vilifies its opponents, and
thrives on never-ending conflict, it has been co-opted by the
world it seeks to change.

Dietrich Bonhoeffer admonished his generation to turn away from ideology. He described ideologues as those "with restless energy" who refuse to take note of resistance and whose actions spring from a confusion of the gospel with a victorious ideology. The greatest danger is that in their preoccupation with the ideological enemy, they lose sight of what the enemy is doing to their own hearts and minds. Bonhoeffer, as others before and after him, worried about the corrupting influence that ideologies and ideological warfare have on the soul of Christians. When the attitudes, methods, and prejudices of the world creep into individuals, they become corrupted by their adversaries and yield control of their actions to others.[6]

Russell Kirk, perhaps the leading American conservative in the twentieth century, has set out to "persuade a rising generation to set their faces against the political fanaticism and utopian schemes" that have plagued the world for much of this century.[7] Conservatives, who have traditionally stood against political ideology, might themselves slip into "a narrow ideology" even though conservatism is best understood as the "negation of ideology." Conservatives cannot offer their own dream of a "terrestrial Paradise that always, in reality, has turned out to be an earthly hell."[8]

Kirk describes ideology as a "snare and a delusion"—an inverted religion—that tries to offer a form of redemption to society that is not possible outside of spiritual transformation. Ideology is the disease, not the cure, and it is "hostile to the enduring order of justice and freedom."[9] Restoration in an age ravaged by ideology can begin when we recognize the need to eliminate ideology's power in society and replace it with an alternative vision based on the facts of history and moral wisdom.

Ideological movements have little restorative power and often only reflect the fragmented and weakened society to which they are reacting. David Walsh has said that a civilization is in a state of crisis "not when its order has broken down for one reason or another, but when the attempt to restore the authoritative order of society is itself ineffective and thereby serves only to exacerbate the original problem."[10]

Power cannot transform human nature and will not win the culture wars. Attempts to so use it could fulfill the dream of those who would completely politicize, and thus destabilize, society. Because ideology is a source of disorder, faith should not be made its ally. The greatest need is for faith to restore the culture based on what Dawson describes at "a power of its own order."[11] True religion, as Kirk notes, is discipline of the soul, not the state.

#3: PURSUE JUSTICE FOR ALL, NOT "JUST US"

Public action should start with a desire to act charitably toward all people. The good society should be based on the highest principles of justice and the public good. The term justice embodies the universal ideals of freedom, fairness, and moral equality that should guide a free society. The abuse and disuse of the term explains in large part why so much public action appears to be little more than the pursuit of private interests or the political advantage of a specific group, rather than the pursuit of a more just society for all.

People of faith must be students of justice. When public action is committed to a pursuit of justice, it is guided by a higher commitment than simply winning a victory for one's own side. By definition, justice raises particular issues to be matters of public interest, not just private concern. Using justice as a frame of reference in public debate can safeguard activists from views and appeals that appear narrow and self-seeking. The pursuit of justice provides many opportunities for exemplary individual action.

American society continues to fall short of the highest standards of compassion and justice. Government certainly has an obligation to protect citizens from violence, establish ethical standards in a host of areas, and administer the law fairly. But the American experience is proof of government's dramatic limitations to accomplish the good and just society by itself. Having one of the most litigious and costly legal systems has destroyed voluntary conflict resolution and failed to make Americans significantly more secure in their rights. A generous welfare system may have secured redistributive justice for poor people, but it has left them socially incompetent and dependent.

Individual Americans must apply standards of fairness, equality, and impartiality in all aspects of life, through private actions as well as public policy. Government cannot be omnipresent in a society that wishes to remain free. Thus the call to administer justice is a call to penetrate the entire marketplace of human exchange—in family life, economics, the environment, law, and medicine to name a few. And it is a call for voluntary action to protect the weak and vulnerable—the unborn, orphans, widows, abused women and children, and the poor.

#4: BE CITIZENS, NOT TRIBESPEOPLE

Some aspects of what passes for religious political activism is simply not very Christian. There is no scriptural justification for an "interest group" model of politics that implies that the interests, rights, or political demands of believers provide the raison d'être for their politics. And there is no basis for conduct or speech that projects resentment, spite, or slander. Nor is there a basis for advancing a limited concept of justice and righteousness.

American democracy's orientation toward group power has become prominent in recent years. So dominant are organized groups in the electoral process that some have described the American political system as "interest-group democracy." Other observers believe the proliferation and dominance of interest groups broadens democratic participation in this highly technical and specialized society, which has become less accessible to ordinary citizens. Many more fear that interest-group domination represents a form of balkanization that could undo democracy itself.

What no one has suggested is that interest-group power supplies society and its democratic institutions with the transcendence it needs to maintain harmony and cohesion. There is a powerful impulse for Christian Americans to take a chapter out of secular politics and organize as just another interest group; to act like another "tribe." The problem with tribal politics, however, is that the model of action forms the members' perceptions. For the Christian tribe, the result is an advancement of its own interests rather than the promotion of a broad vision for society.

Tribal politics only reinforces attitudes that are both wrong and counterproductive. It reinforces the sense of fear and anger that many feel over having their dominant space in society invaded by other influences. Tribal politics encourages methods of action that are designed to produce tribal solidarity so to counter the assault coming from outside. Rarely are methods examined for their consistency with their claims.

The more compelling model for public participation is the citizen model. Here the church is simply called to serve society, not as conditions require but because of God's demands. Politics is thus but one facet of this calling. The citizen translates faith into a public philosophy, seeks to build inclusive coalitions around a broad agenda, and prefers persuasion to polarization. This has broader possibilities for pursuing the cleanup of the moral environment than does traditional politics.

Tribal politics huddles and confronts the hostile world with a hostility that only mirrors its antagonists and resists evaluating its own conduct and methods. Citizen participation, in contrast, assimilates and strives to advance a common vision for the common good.

This citizen approach to advancing values has several distinct advantages over tribal politics. First, it starts with an acknowledgment of pluralism—that our land has a rich religious and social diversity and that society belongs to all of its members. Although refusing to accept some views, true citizens never deny the basic moral worth of each human being nor believe they have a special divine dispensation to rule over others.

Second, this citizen approach of a pluralistic model helps social activists overcome insularity. The isolation of many traditionalists fosters behavior and attitudes that are counterproductive to their own objectives, such as the pointless hairsplitting and endless bickering, the presumption that Americans wish to be led by those who narrowcast the values debate, and the dark suspicions toward those who simply disagree. Movements that organize themselves around an "us versus them" mentality ensure that disputes are raised to the level of insurmountable disagreement.

Third, the citizen model trains and encourages individuals to act responsibly on their own at all levels of society, without suggesting that they need to be organized behind a person, faction, party, or polarizing labels. Many activist organizations push factional politics for their own unstated reasons: their funding and institutional successes depend on being seen as a power broker. But polarizing tactics change very few people. Instead they solidify the opposing positions that existed prior to engagement, reinforcing their own social and political isolation. A takeover will only occur when principled and competent people rise to the top—much like Daniel in Babylon—through superior wisdom, integrity, and skill. It will come by projecting broad visions, earning the right to be heard, being modest in one's own confidence and abilities, and, simply, by earning the respect of majorities.

Fourth, the citizen model discourages the belief that cultural conflicts are resolvable through political and legislative action alone. It recognizes politics as a critical battleground for many important issues as well as an important platform for debating values, but sees political action as a subsidiary of a larger realm in society.

#5: ADD SOCIAL COMPASSION TO THE MORAL MANDATE

People of faith must become people of social conscience again. Because the Christian church's public witness is no longer linked to social action, with a few notable exceptions, its moral pronouncements often lack moral authority.

The tragic result of the compartmentalization of faith that excludes social responsibility is a movement away from the very centers of opportunity for impact. For example, one of the greatest opportunities for coalition building lies with the black community, whose members have a church attendance rate as high as 80 percent. But the barrier to greater cooperation is hindered by white conservatives' social indifference on issues of race and civil rights as well as the flight of middle-class churches from urban neighborhoods.

History supplies us with repeated examples of how social and political reform follows, or at least accompanies, spiritual reform. Many of the greatest social reforms were, in fact, created by religious revival. The great revivals in Europe and America not only converted individuals but fueled social reform on both sides of the Atlantic.

The revivals led by John Wesley and George Whitefield in the American colonies not only produced a great turning to God but influenced the American Revolution and the birth of the nation. J. Wesley Bready has described revival as "the true nursing mother of the spirit and values that created and sustained free institutions throughout the English speaking world." Revivalism and social reform went hand in hand.[12]

Reform also accompanied revival during the early 1800s. Charles Finney's drive for spiritual renewal was accompanied by a passion of equal intensity to reform the world. The business of the church, according to Finney, was to fight for reformation of the world as well as the reformation of souls. Not surprisingly, his revival movement raised up an army of young activists who led the reform movements of his time, including the movement to eradicate slavery. According to historian Timothy Smith, "Charles Finney probably won as many converts to the cause as William Lloyd Garrison, even though he shunned the role of agitator for that of winner of souls."[13] Religious movements strongly opposed slavery but were more caught up in the spiritual current of abolitionism than in abolitionist parties. The church

was engaged in building missions, hospitals, schools, and charities to meet the needs of the poor.

Another historical example shows the relationship between
revival and social reform. American urban conditions in the late
nineteenth century were just as despairing as today. Thousands of
orphans roamed the streets of New York City. Infant mortality
rates were 10 times the present levels. Prostitutes and opium
slaves lined the streets.

New York City's war on poverty was led by the charitable
action of religious groups and individuals, not by government
social agencies. The stories told by eyewitnesses are remarkable—one reformer told of forty-five hundred families being
raised out of pauperism over an eight-year period and sixty thousand children being rescued from the streets and given homes.
Churches provided meals, training in basic skills, and temporary lodging if necessary. The churches also dramatically reduced
abortion—which at the time was almost as high per capita as it
is now—by applying social rather than legislative strategies.[14]

In the past, the churches provided the breakthroughs
because they offered a special antibody into the decaying corpse
of America's ghettoes: a fundamental change in character and
conduct rooted in spiritual transformation. Unlike what some
advocate, programs and economics cannot touch the roots of
the disorder in our cities.

Glenn Loury, professor of economics at Boston University,
recognizes this and describes the urban crisis as "a disease of the
soul for which a more powerful balm than money will be
required. . . . Through our government, our churches and our civil
society, we must—all of us—be in relationship with them. . . .
The point here transcends politics and policy. It is a spiritual
point of the highest order."[15]

These historical examples remind us of the times when social
reform was promoted by spiritual revivals. Today the church is
mostly known for its public mistakes, many of which emanate
from popular myths about public life. One myth is to assume
that vice and decay are unique features of the late twentieth

century and that vice is predominantly corrected by legislative change rather than individual and social reform. Another is to believe that social decay can be easily, quickly, and painlessly eradicated. Those searching for quick fixes need to learn that change comes over long periods of time, produced through patience and perseverance.

People of faith today must make a greater effort to understand how the world works and how they can be faithful in changing it. Whereas many revivalists and reformers throughout the centuries devoted themselves to building foundations that would produce renewal over the course of decades, many of today's leaders cannot see beyond the first hundred days of an incoming administration in Washington.

This outlook produces what John Stott has called "an air of rather self-righteous dismay." "We bewail the world's deteriorating standards . . . we criticize its violence, dishonesty, immorality, disregard for human life, and materialistic greed." But we do this without realizing that not only has the world been deteriorating for a long time, but it has also been renewing itself through the courageous and sacrificial service of Spirit-led reformers. The surging revival has emanated from churches—not legislatures, courts, or political parties.

True empowerment in today's spiritually impoverished and socially fragmented world may come in the form of spiritual renewal. Although religion has been assumed by many to be irrelevant in modern secularized, rationalized, bureaucratized society, doors of opportunity for religious influence may be opening once again.

CONCLUSION

Politics is at its best when it reflects an awareness of its inadequacies. Politics, by itself, can do little to save our cities, end teen pregnancy, or significantly reduce crime, drugs, or poverty. Legislative action is not the answer for encouraging people to learn, excel, save, or invest, to name a few. That requires changes in human conduct and character.

Political and religious activists have simply put too much confidence in power and their capacity to use it for the greater good. America does not need a political revolution, it needs a behavioral revolution. And behavioral change is not imposed, it is cultivated.

Can faith once again engage society on a broad scale, igniting fundamental change? The record of history suggests that it can, and that it possesses perhaps the only real antidote to spiritual and social disorder.

Abraham Kuyper served as prime minister in the Netherlands from 1901 to 1905 and dedicated his life to encouraging and guiding Christian reformation of church and society. He was driven by a sense of Christian calling and a conviction that piety was not a private affair. He wrote: "The fellowship of being near unto God must become reality, in the full and vigorous prosecution of our life. It must permeate and give color to our feeling, our perceptions, our sensations, our thinking our imagining, our willing, our acting, our speaking."[16]

This sense that all of life must be lived for God opens all vocations to the possibility for spiritual influence. But understanding all of life to be religious does not mean that Christians should confuse civil authority with ecclesiastical authority. We must not confuse society and the state, nor the divine authority that extends over believers in the church with the civil authority that extends over citizens through the government.

Politics is a subsidiary of the higher and more important sphere of civil society. Thus believers must permeate society. Christians need to live with integrity and make distinctive contributions in the social, scientific, artistic, educational, and political life of the nation.

Religion, society, and politics constantly interact, but occupy differing spheres. Creating a healthy cultural and political order will not come through politicized religion or religionized politics. Religion is at its best when it gently prods the heart to faith, molds the mind to create, and bends the will to do great works. And politics is at its best when it is not only undergirded by Christian ethics, but committed to serving the common good of all.

10

RENEWING AMERICA'S CIVIC VISION

TODAY AMERICANS FACE momentous challenges and change at a dizzying pace. George Gallup has described the profound shifts in American society as a "great historical tidal wave—a set of monumental political, social and economic impulses, which are carrying us relentlessly toward a rendezvous with the future."[1]

Suddenly Americans are turning inward and asking fresh questions: What is the state of our values and democratic institutions? Can the country that is the birthplace of modern liberty remain a world leader if current trends continue? As old belief systems collapse, a contest of wills and ideas will determine the social and political contours of the twenty-first century. Perhaps as never in our history, Americans will have to summon forth strength based on our inner character and resolve.

In September 1863, Abraham Lincoln dedicated a cemetery to young soldiers who gave the full measure of devotion in the war. The question Lincoln asked on that solemn occasion is the question that devoted patriots should ask today: "Can this nation, or any nation so conceived and so dedicated, long endure?" Many are searching anew for what the content of a nation's character and values must be for freedom to endure. Many citizens sense that America is encountering a new and different threat—this one from within.

One of the central arguments in this book has been that what the dialectical materialism of the former communist world did not destroy, and could not destroy because of the West's determined resistance, a different form of materialism—this one secular, democratic, and largely unresisted—has steadily moved to accomplish. The moral apathy and indifference of the West may prove to be a more deadly plague on the life of the spirit than the most brutal form of totalitarianism.

The societies of the West lie in a state of spiritual anomie—a condition just as threatening to humanity as the physical threat of a foreign adversary. Whereas threats of devastation or oppression are tolerable when there are transcendent explanations, even mild threats can become unbearable when the structures of beliefs and meaning crumble.

The battle to restore the basic ideas and values of the American experiment will be profoundly different than previous conflicts and challenges Americans have faced. Such questions as the following will need to be raised: What foundations exist to provide for the restoration of badly weakened public institutions and civil society? How can urgently needed reform be advanced in a political process dominated by interests strongly resistant to reform? How can basic American philosophical principles be restored without simply advancing other ideologies that compete for power? How can one restore a culture, along with its institutions and professions, without resorting to statism and demagoguery? In a society dominated by what David Walsh describes as a "modernist impulse to throw off restraints and religious authority," how does one restore values without being perceived as "one more reactionary attempt to assert religious controls"?[2] How does one go about restoring religion to its proper place in society?

Restoring the good society will neither be easy nor simple, for promoting a social and spiritual reformation is complex. But there are important steps we must take. These two concluding chapters will put forward important themes and objectives needed to foster a restoration. This chapter will focus on the necessary renewal of democratic ideals and the final chapter will explore five key areas in the lives of American citizens that need such renewal.

#1: THE RESTORATION OF DEMOCRATIC INSTITUTIONS: TOTAL INTEGRITY POLITICS

The convulsions that have hit so many of America's institutions are particularly rocking politics. The biggest movements in 1992—Ross Perot's unsuccessful bid for president and successful term-limit initiatives in over a dozen states—both operated almost entirely outside of traditional party politics. This suggests that today's real revolt is against the business of politics itself.

People find politics remote because it has evolved into a highly calibrated business in which a fairly permanent governing class is both the producer and consumer. The public, not surprisingly, sees politicians as serving their own purposes, more prone to create than solve crises, and less likely to supply real solutions for improving the quality of life. Americans are hostile toward and removed from what Perot called "an expensive sideshow": a spectacle of political careerism, pointless polarization, and interest-group gridlock.

Men and women of principle must move to restore lost integrity in our nation's political and governmental institutions. Steps must be taken to promote a form of political leadership that speaks not only candidly and clearly to America's growing moral disorder, but sensitively, realizing the limitations of power to resolve issues that represent deep conflicts over basic assumptions.

Politics must be freed from its excessive entanglement with the dominant interests and ideological preoccupations that prevent it from articulating and advancing clearly defined national interests. Our nation's capital today is home to over twenty thousand registered lobbyists, four thousand associations, and four thousand political action committees (PACs), the vast majority of which are dedicated to the enrichment of a particular group at the expense of the general public. Interest-group domination is even worse in many state capitals, where government is often little more than a referee that oversees the contest between organized groups.

Above all, politics cannot be left to career political professionals. Incumbent officeholders symbolize a politics that is devoid of competition, dominated by interests, funded by PACs, and padded with perks. Even today's political parties, which were born of noble purposes, focus primarily on electing and keeping elected the home team—with little accountability ever imposed. With a few notable exceptions, entering political office today resembles an ancient tribal ritual in which the inductee leaves one society to join another. With the act of joining comes a new tribal attitude—master the game of self-preservation. Stay in office for life, by whatever means necessary.

Tragically, the success of political careerists comes at the expense of a vibrant democracy, led by citizen politicians. The founders shared an antipathy toward any trace of aristocracy appearing on the American scene. Ben Franklin said, "In free governments, the rulers are the servants and the people their superiors. For the former, to return among the latter does not degrade, but promote them."[3]

If the framers saw how a professionalized politics now undermines genuine representation, many believe they would recommend more binding methods of turnover to ensure that the leaders returned to live among the led. But although blunt instruments, such as mandatory term-limits, might satisfy an alienated public's hunger to strike back, mere turnover would not necessarily restore honor to the profession of politics. The business of politics itself is the central issue, not the length of service.

What is most needed in the American political process is the renewal of politics from within. If the threat of international competition produced a movement toward Total Quality Management in business, perhaps the threat of upheaval of American society could produce Total Integrity Politics—a new bipartisan renewal movement.

The core theme of Total Integrity Politics would be simple: given the corrosion of public trust, if something in politics appears to lack integrity then it probably does and should be stopped. Congressional Representatives, for example, are not seen as public servants because they pay themselves over a hundred thirty thousand dollars in salary. Public respect for state legislators will be difficult to regain so long as they use ingenious backdoor methods to compensate themselves. Citizens who would contribute financially to campaigns may not believe their contributions have any influence because of PAC contributions. These are all examples of areas that Total Integrity Politics could transform.

Total Integrity Politics could promote a new burst of honesty. Public cynicism is rooted in the fact that while government has underperformed, politics has been oversold. Political agendas—on both the Left and the Right—have been dramatically exaggerated as sources of national renewal. Politicians should not make the stakes appear higher than ever merely to stay in office.

In reality, the stakes on many policy issues are low, particularly because foreign policy concerns have diminished with the demise of communism. Though great divisions will continue over moral issues, tax policy, and judicial appointments, the vast majority of issues will focus on the means, not the ends—how to deliver education, welfare, health care, and so on. Moreover, the most powerful symbol of political oversell—the deficit—will guarantee that no matter what is promised in politics, much less will be done.

A wise use of political office would simply be to communicate that if we are going to save families, make our neighborhoods friendly and safe, and restore such lost virtues as honesty and civility, than we, the people, must do it. Politicians cannot rebuild the lost community—only citizens can. But politicians' honest words and mediating influence can steer society in this direction.

All of this takes us back to the central point: People desire a new politics that is honest, unpretentious, and restored to its proper dimension. The greatest hope of Americans may be to live in a society that is less splintered by race, class, and divisive politics. Politics, as we know it, injures—not heals—society. The question is, can it change?

Communitarian leader Amitai Etzioni argues that producing change in government by simply "throwing the rascals out" and replacing them with new leaders does not take into account today's systemic problems. The next batch will be just as beholden to social movements as the previous group. Etzioni argues for a new turn-of-the-century "progressive" movement whose aim would be to restore lost integrity. Unlike the nineteenth-century progressive movement that aimed to reduce the large concentrations of wealth and political power following industrialization, this movement would reduce the concentrated power of politically entrenched interest groups.[4]

#2: THE RESTORATION OF CITIZENSHIP: THE INDIVIDUAL AS THE AGENT OF CHANGE

People need to be restored to full participation in the whole of public life. Whatever blame politicians may face for the dismal state of America's public life and institutions, renewal will come when the people themselves are determined to produce it. For government, as James Madison said, is "the greatest of all reflections on human nature." In many ways it is a mirror of our own lives.

As George Bernard Shaw has said, democracy is a device "that ensures we shall be governed no better than we deserve." Tocqueville warned of American democracy feeding on itself—degenerating into clamoring mobs who vote for themselves every favor and demand rights and privileges for the few while overlooking duty to society. Though politicians have polished the fine art of pandering, the demand for rights and entitlements has been a constant refrain coming from the people. James Q. Wilson has described these popular expectations in unflattering terms. Every poll taken over the last few decades shows that "large majorities think that the federal government taxes too heavily, spends too little, that deficit financing is wrong, and that Washington should solve problems that no state or local government has been able to solve."[5]

The $300 billion annual deficit resulting from this deep contradiction is not likely to disappear by simply doing away with a little "waste, fraud, and abuse," as many Americans naively suppose. There is no lack of government today, nor is there a great abundance of individual responsibility. The absence of the latter may explain the great supply of the former. Change, at least of the kind that America needs most badly, will come from the people.

It is time to stop complaining about public problems and start rebuilding the quality of our public life. Harry Boyte, author of *CommonWealth: A Return to Citizen Politics*, says it is time to reinvent citizenship. "If something is wrong, we as citizens must make it right."[6] Citizenship should not be sentimentalized because it involves sacrificial contributions through hard work.

Whether the importance and independence of citizenship was taken away by politicians or simply relinquished by the people is now irrelevant. Whatever government does or does not do, the job of restoration and renewal will fall heavily to the citizens. Citizenship will be restored when people recognize the limitations of political action to solve our deepest social problems.

William Raspberry has summed it up well:

School reform cannot educate black children who equate academic exertion with "acting white." No jobs program will cure income problems of people who believe that the "chump change" rewards of entry level work are beneath them. No system of health care, no matter how freely available, will improve the health of people who persist in such risky behavior as drug abuse, bad eating habits or promiscuous sex. . . no housing subsidy will deliver home ownership to people who refuse to save or who insist on having too many children too soon.[7]

Resuscitating an older, deeper, fuller concept of citizenship requires that individuals must be seen as capable of self-government by both themselves and their leaders. Indeed, responsibility must be made the cornerstone again of America's basic social contract. There is scant hope for change based on top-down strategies, impersonal theories, or programmatic reforms. America will be changed one family and one neighborhood at a time, through individual initiative. Citizens must take responsibility for nourishing institutions, imparting character, and rediscovering timeless wisdom for daily life.

Philanthropist Michael Joyce has outlined what a new citizenship would entail compared to its current shrunken definition. Today's understanding of citizenship is defined almost entirely in terms of political activity, especially voting. When politicians appeal to individuals to exercise citizenship, they mean "come out and vote for us so we can do something for you." Empowerment, in this case, flows upward from the people to politicians and professionals. According to Joyce, the chief purpose of this form of citizenship is first to vote, then to "turn over to supposedly qualified experts the real business of public life, namely, designing and launching public programs of all sorts, which will bestow upon the victims of poverty or AIDS or discrimination or some other insidious force the tender mercies of bureaucrats, policy experts, social therapists and others, who claim to be uniquely able to cope with such problems by virtue of professional training."[8]

An expert class has asserted cultural hegemony over much of American life, robbing individual Americans of their status as true citizens and reducing them to the status of clients. In search of problems to convert to programs, this expert class looks on ordinary people—their values, religion, and commitment to common sense—with condescension.

The chief objective of the new citizenship would be to reclaim the individual from the clutches of imperial elites. True citizens would refuse to delegate the business of public life to professionals. Instead they would see the individuals who serve as good neighbors, volunteers, and sources of private charity as the very lifeblood of the society.

This notion of citizenship encourages people to emerge from extreme individualism and reenter community—a spiritual community of sorts that links them in partnership with the past and the future. For society, in Edmund Burke's words, is a spiritual community, a partnership "in all science, a partnership in all art, a partnership in every virtue. . . ." This partnership is obtained not only "between those who are living, but between those who are living, those who are dead, and those who are yet to be born."[9]

Social renewal based on citizenship will require our removing inward and outward barriers to empowerment. Inward barriers consist of people's refusal to take responsibility, determination to cling to the claims of victimhood, and willingness to accept client status in a therapeutic state. These inward barriers are often the product of missing hope, an aching alienation, and a lack of faith. Those interested in a renewed society must be interested in personal rejuvenation, for a society's spiritual exterior is only a reflection of individuals' spiritual interior. Outward barriers consist of any impediment to achieving full participation in society, whether in politics, economics, or civic life. It means removing roadblocks to political efficacy, barriers to self-sufficiency, and obstacles to economic opportunity.

Those committed to citizenship will understand that problems exist and sometimes will require public help. Many barriers to citizenship and self-sufficiency are real. Some individuals, for instance, lack the values necessary to profit from economic opportunity. But there are also many motivated individuals who lack basic resources and opportunities. Bill Clinton generated much sympathy during his campaign by repeating: "There are a lot of people who have the values right, and everything continues to go wrong."

A restoration of citizenship ultimately requires a new commitment to the common good. Russell Kirk described the principal components of good citizenship as "moderation, social sympathy and willingness to sacrifice private desires for public ends."[10]

#3: The Restoration of Civil Society: Decentralist Republicanism

Citizenship entails a range of social duties that are carried out through associational life. This is civil society, the realm in which individuals conduct much of their lives. A well-functioning society should be made up of what Burke called "little platoons,"[11] Emile Durkheim called "the little aggregations,"[12] and Christopher Dawson called the "interpenetrating orders—political, economic, cultural and religious."[13] Each order should possess a considerable amount of independence.

The same point was established in our own generation by Peter L. Berger and Richard John Neuhaus. Their little classic *To Empower People* put the term "mediating structures" on the map. By mediating structures they mean above all the institutions, such as families, churches and synagogues, voluntary associations, and neighborhoods, that come between the world of the individual and the world of the state. "*Mediating structures,*" they argued, "*are essential for a vital democratic society. . . . Public policy should protect and foster mediating structures, and Whenever possible, public policy should utilize mediating structures for the realization of social purposes.*"[14] The result of healthy mediating structures, they argued, would be empowerment.

All of these aspects of voluntary exchange make up civil society. As Michael Joyce wrote recently, civil society

> encompasses all the institutions through which individuals express their interests and values, outside of and distinct from government. Thus, it includes our activities in the marketplace, including acquiring private property, holding a job, and earning a living. It includes what we do as loving members of our family; as students or concerned parents within our schools; as worshipful attendees of our churches; and as faithful mem-

bers of neighborhood associations, clubs, fraternal and sororal lodges, and ethnic voluntary associations of all sorts.[15]

The continuous interaction with these mediating institutions shapes community life. The vast majority of social needs are still met through these associational ties, even in the midst of a large central welfare state. Many of the functions of the state are best delegated to this sector of American life, not only to limit government's growth but also to preserve the health of civic institutions.

Strong civil institutions curb both the growth of government and ameliorate individual needs by passing on to succeeding generations such values as self-restraint, perseverance, and honesty. Says Joyce, "Through our vast, complex web of civil institutions, in short, we grow and develop into complete human beings—learning to suppress our often chaotic and destructive impulses; to express our connectedness and mutual obligation to each other; to reach beyond ourselves, so to speak, to higher aspirations, reflecting nobler impulses."[16]

These mediating structures of human society are unique in that they belong fully to the people to organize and regulate—not to the state or professional elites. Thus they are the most important structures for a free people to maintain. Although these institutions preserve our highest ideals and thus are vital to nourish, they are the first to come under assault from the many forces of culture.

Robert Nisbet has argued that civil society is assaulted from below and above. The authority of such institutions as family, church, neighborhood, and school are slowly weakened from below by the proliferation of individual rights. Civil institutions are pressured from above to surrender authority and function to the professional elites of the centralized, bureaucratized state. The voluntary associations of civil society cannot match the power of individualism asserted from below or the power of bureaucratic centralization operating from above.[17]

Only through the commitments of millions of Americans can voluntary associations be preserved. Americans themselves will have to resist the steady loss of civic autonomy by fortifying local associations and institutions against the assaults from above or below. By curbing both individualism and bureaucratization, Americans can preserve community life. Policy makers can reinforce the strength of local community life and its problem-solving capacity by both decentralizing public programs and expanding the role of the private sector—particularly churches, civic groups, and charities.

#4: THE RESTORATION OF THE PUBLIC PHILOSOPHY: A SHARED VISION FOR THE COMMON GOOD

Abraham Lincoln, traveling to his inauguration in 1861, delivered a speech before an audience assembled in Independence Hall. He said, "All the political sentiments I entertain have been drawn from the sentiments which originated and were given to the world from this hall. I have never had a feeling politically that did not spring from the sentiments embodied in the Declaration of Independence."

The greatest expressions of the American idea were not filled with the arcane jargon of economics or governmentalism. They have been about self-evident truths and ideals that Americans uniquely treasure. They resonate with the grand vision that the occupants of this land, though they come from almost everywhere else, are here to fill a unique place in "the course of human events."

As Americans search for a definition of purpose, they should look to the content of their creed. G. K. Chesterton, who visited America during the 1920s, concluded that "America was the only nation in the world that was founded on a creed."[18] Without the factors of race, ancestry, ethnicity, or nationalism to build on, this creed has filled the imagination and kept democracy vibrant. What has fueled American greatness is an idea that must not only be publicly promoted but made concrete in the lives of Americans.

The creed consists of many things: the uniquely American idea of progress and special destiny, equality, liberty, optimism, and boundless opportunity. Many of these ideals are embodied in the stories and myths that are told and retold by one generation to the next. These myths, and the dreams and ideals enshrined in them, supply a unifying force. And it is this American mythology that is too frequently undermined by what Peggy Noonan calls "the compulsive skepticism of the modern mind."

It has long been assumed that this nation could handle any amount of diversity, provided the American idea remained the universal creed of all. All that the American creed required was that the new waves of immigrants be "Americanized"; that they accept the American creed. But Arthur Schlesinger, Jr. wonders if America is pulling apart, not only segregating once more into separate ethnic and racial enclaves, but withdrawing from the American creed.

Those who discount the importance of these ideals fail to appreciate their role in making one nation out of many. The public philosophy, which Os Guinness describes as a shared vision for the common good, embraces liberty for individuals, tolerance for America's ethnic mosaic, and a well-moderated pluralism. But it finds its real strength in what Americans have in common in public life.

A return to a strong public philosophy can heal a land divided by race, class, religion, and ideology. On race and class, it can offer a vision for shared progress based on upward mobility through expanded opportunity and targeted measures to empower the poor. On issues of religion and ideology, its rediscovery can restore the early synthesis of biblical religion and classical philosophy that made not only the founding of the republic possible, but its periodic renewal as well.

Daniel Bell sees America as held together by an implicit covenant, which from the beginning was based on a sense that "this was the continent where God's design would be unfolded." Though this original idea of covenant has receded somewhat as a more "open, adaptive, egalitarian, and democratic system" has been built, it remains a core theme in inspiring a sense of common commitment in American democracy.[19]

#5: The Restoration of American Culture: Penetrating the Value-Shaping Institutions

Cultural and political liberals understand that government is a secondary arena for shaping society. They know that the media, education, academia, and the elite professions play the primary roles. Traditionalists, in contrast, understand the realm of culture mostly as a target for political attack, not a realm to enter and shape. If conservatives do not overcome their anti-intellectualism and fear and disdain for the creative order of ideas, it is doubtful that their influence in any arena—even politics—will grow. For in the final analysis, cultural and political conflicts are won by winning hearts and minds.

Religious conservatives, in particular, have not influenced culture because the entire enterprise of culture-shaping, as contrasted to lawmaking, is simply not regarded as spiritual. "Loving not the things of this world" is translated into contempt for the world, except apparently in the concrete world of legislation where issues appear in more black and white terms. But fondness for the power of ideas in politics is no substitute for the greater power of ideas in culture.

The drift toward personal rootlessness, cultural nihilism, and the erosion of the transcendent foundations of society all emanate from the highest levels of American culture. The decline of traditional Western ideas can be traced to developments in art, literature, philosophy, and other disciplines. For it is in the humanities where deconstructionism and the political correctness movement have been most deeply rooted. But it is also in this arena where the proponents of traditional values have been most absent, apparently lacking the time or temperament, or both. Passion for fighting the culture wars in the arena of populist politics apparently does not extend to the painstaking support for traditional culture in academia.

Although high culture may be beyond the reach of most, mass culture is as open to influence as politics, and far more influential. For instance, radio and television play a profoundly important role in shaping the values of youth, as any parent or educator knows. In a recent survey documenting the most influential role models for kids, the athletes, entertainers, and other stars of popular culture held sway. The only politician who made it on the list was not even American—it was Nelson Mandela of South Africa.

The generation that mounts a serious restoration of American society will include on its agenda a vision for cultural reclamation—of both elite and mass culture. As Plato said, "Give me the songs of a nation, and it matters not who writes its laws." A nation's manners and morals are more important than the law. This is the business of culture.

11

ESTABLISHING THE NATIONAL PRIORITIES

To RESTORE THE GOOD SOCIETY we must not only renew commitment to democratic ideals, as we explored in the previous chapter, but we must revitalize five key areas in the lives of citizens. These include the professions, education, social movements, the family, and faith.

#1: THE RESTORATION OF PROFESSIONS: MARKETPLACE ETHICS

A vital area of needed restoration is in permeating the key professions with a new commitment to excellence and ethics. Professionals have far greater access to the centers of cultural and political power than individuals, and thus can have an impact for good well out of proportion to their numbers.

Business leaders should understand the relationship between culture and economics, because it is the quality of human resources that increasingly affects profits in our information-based global marketplace. Values and character, or the lack thereof, have costly consequences for the workplace and economy. For example, the absence of individual responsibility accounts for hundreds of billions of dollars in taxes for government expenditures that could have been avoided if values were maintained.

For Adam Smith, capitalism was much more than a value-free engine of wealth creation. Free-market capitalism was assumed to work in the context of a human civilization that believed that traditional morality would discipline self-interest. Today, as one corporate executive remarked, "the national principles that undergird a functional, productive life seem to be fast disappearing."

A democratic regime based entirely on commercial self-interest is by no means "an edifying spectacle," according to political scientist Bill Schambra. Its citizens "can be selfish, narrow, materialistic, grasping and small-minded; its politicians self-aggrandizing and shortsighted."[1]

This description could be applied to many professionals who have reduced their honorable fields to little more than a chase for bigger paychecks. The Protestant work ethic has been replaced, according to Daniel Bell, "by a culture compulsively concerned with play, fun, display and pleasure." Now "the old Protestant heavenly virtues are largely gone, and the mundane rewards have begun to run riot."[2]

Lawyers, to name one profession, bear serious culpability for undermining the integrity of the legal system and for a deepening cynicism toward professions in general. The legal profession wields an immense amount of power not only over professionals but also the legal and judicial arenas in which their trade is applied. Reform of the profession will thus have to come from within, as conscientious attorneys renew their commitment to combine professional profitability with a determined pursuit of the public interest.

Much of the medical community, to name another professional area, pays little more than lip service to the Hippocratic oath, leaving the public increasingly distrustful of placing their lives and health under the stewardship of medical professionals. Perhaps if medical associations cannot reaffirm their commitment to the dignity and worth of all human life, a breakaway group should form to confer a seal of approval on physicians who do. Interested consumers could learn of their philosophy and the availability of their services.

Perhaps the greatest need for professional reform lies in the category of education. Whereas teachers once focused primarily on shaping what happens in the classroom, national teacher unions are now the most powerful groups in shaping education policy and politics. The National Education Association's platform is more extreme than the vast majority of America's teachers. These teachers should not stand for the continued erosion of public confidence and respect. The job of responsible educators is nothing short of restoring the teaching profession to its once noble position, restoring virtue, character, and competence to their rightful place at the center of education, and completely depoliticizing the educational enterprise.

#2: THE RESTORATION OF EDUCATION: PARENT POWER AND PHILOSOPHICAL PURPOSE

If educationalists as a profession cry out for dramatic reform, so too does the public education system itself. The need is urgent, for cultural and academic literacy are vital in today's world. Since the Sputnik crisis, we have been experimenting with educational reform as recommended by expert commissions. The experts have advocated to spend more money, boost the pay and training of teachers, improve teacher pupil ratios, and experiment with a host of other institutional reforms. Americans spent $425 billion on education in 1992—far more than the Pentagon's budget—and up from $165 billion just a decade before. National per pupil expenditures average six thousand dollars annually, or one hundred fifty thousand dollars per classroom. Although expenditures have skyrocketed, such test scores as SAT scores remain stagnant or in decline.[3]

But what is worse than slumping test scores is the continuing failure of schools toward fulfilling their moral and philosophical mission in a democratic society. Education has failed to fill young hearts with a passion for life and learning or minds with imagination. The counterculture rebellion of the sixties has produced a climate in which irreverence, skepticism, and mockery permeate scholarship and culture. But this is only one source of the problem. There is little room left today for the respect of adults, pursuit of excellence, or high regard for heroes.

Educator Peter Gibbon says he is terrified that our children "are not being raised by exemplary lives and confident schools; nor by high culture, vigilant communities, families, churches and temples, but rather by an all-enveloping enemy culture interested in amusement, titillation, and consumerism."[4]

The basic need of a free society is to preserve the ideals and values by which free men and women order their lives. Education is not meeting this need. Consider the findings of recent polls. In a Louis Harris poll of five thousand young people, 65 percent said they would cheat to pass an exam and 53 percent said they would lie to protect a friend who had vandalized school property.[5] In a different study, 67 percent of high school seniors said they would inflate an expense account, 50 percent would pad an insurance claim, and 66 percent said they would willingly lie to achieve a business objective.[6]

This disturbing mentality goes to the fundamental issue of truth and its status in a relativistic culture. One of the Harris questions was: "What do you take to be the most believable authority in matters of truth?" Less than 2 percent said science or the media. Slightly less than 4 percent said religion or their parents. Most of the kids simply said "me."[7]

Schools must shoulder a major responsibility for imparting ethical values; the brunt of the absence of values can be easily seen in the schools first. Former Secretary of Education William J. Bennett has said that in the 1940s teachers identified talking out of turn, chewing gum, making noise, running in the halls, cutting in line, dress-code infractions, and littering as their leading concerns. But in the nineties drug and alcohol abuse, pregnancy, suicide, rape, robbery, and assault head the list.

Schools cannot be blamed for the collapse of other value-shaping institutions, such as the family, nor for an epidemic of ethical relativism that is society-wide. Nevertheless, no movement to restore American democracy, civil society, or ethical

standards will be effective if it fails to reform education funda-
mentally.

The entire notion of public education must be redefined to
include education that serves these purposes. What really matters
is whether children are learning, scoring high on tests, getting
into college, and preparing to compete internationally. The basic
tools for democratic life need to be put in place. What matters
less than the institutional structure is the learning that takes
place.

It is rather peculiar that a society so steeped in free enterprise, which regularly condemns private monopolies and praises
choice and competition, would so fervently embrace a state-
dominated system to deliver such a vital service to our democratic society and economic well-being. David Kearns, former
Undersecretary of Education, has described today's education
system as "a failed monopoly—bureaucratic, rigid and in
unsteady control of dissatisfied captive markets."[8]

No other enterprise needs to be rethought and redesigned
quite like education. Too many reforms over the past decade
have tinkered at the edges. The fact is, the current system is
obsolete. How is it that as we approach the twenty-first century
we have an education system that was designed in the agrarian
age when 80 percent of the graduates performed roughly the
same tasks for an entire lifetime?

We now live in the age of information and technology. Of all
the mind-numbing inventions of this century, nothing compares
in revolutionary impact to the microchip. Americans can begin
to envision a future in which the world's libraries can be accessed
through a personal computer at home; a future in which any lec-
ture on any subject can be accessed from church, private or
parochial school, or home. This technology enables Americans
to work out of the home, which can reduce the pace of life and
the destructive undermining of family and community.

Technology, once feared as a source of human oppression,
has proven to be the enemy of tyrants and bureaucrats. Technology will revolutionize institutions, particularly such public

institutions as education that have been stiffly resistant to market forces and citizen demands for greater accountability. In time,
the entire public education establishment could find itself just
as defenseless against the democratizing pull of technology as
former East bloc autocrats were defenseless against photocopy
and fax machines.

Control of the philosophy of education is linked to control of
the economics of education. Attempts to reform the philosophy
of education are not likely to succeed until parents are empow-
ered with the ability to guide their child's education directly.

#3: THE RESTORATION OF SOCIAL MOVEMENTS: ADDING SOCIAL ACTION TO POLITICAL ACTION

Many Americans from across the political spectrum see political
activism as the only instrument to change America, even though
public problems at the neighborhood level simply cannot be
fixed by authorities located in some distant place. Growing numbers of elected officials themselves are privately voicing exas-
peration over the limited capacity even of fully funded programs
or fully staffed police departments, social agencies, and prisons to
cope with spiraling social problems.

But it is difficult to imagine significant breakthroughs coming from City Hall or state or federal lawmakers to reduce crime,
teen pregnancy, family fragmentation, dependency on drugs and
alcohol, or the decline in manners and morals. The American
restoration movement must develop strategies for change that, in
some cases, are almost entirely social.

The traditional argument about government's limitations
has been twofold: first, that government is the problem and thus
the solution is simply to get rid of it; second, that by eliminating
government, civic society, individual virtue, and strong local
communities will magically reappear. But this position will strike
many Americans as hopelessly naive in light of our current state
of social disorder.

A more sound view is that the debate over the size of the government should not divide Americans, distracting them from doing what only they can do. Moreover, those on each side of the debate should fortify their arguments by the example of their own lives.

Americans must transcend politics, with its narrow, repetitive, and often pointless debates, and work together to solve problems that are manifestly unsolvable by any amount of government. The debate about "governmentalism"—how much and in what form—has taken place from the beginning of time and will not likely disappear. But even if there were a sudden resolution in this debate, little would change.

What must be recognized is that a great many of America's weaknesses lie in the civic, cultural, and moral realm where government solutions are often deficient and unworkable. David Blankenhorn of the Institute for American Values describes an American "social recession" and a "cultural regression" that have serious consequences for America's future. He says, "There is a declining sense of civic obligation, a lowering of trust in social institutions, a diminution of caring for one another in society, along with the increase of a range of personal pathologies," among which he includes declining mental health, crime, teen suicide, depression, and an assortment of personal maladies.[9]

How can we rebuild confidence in schools, restore neighborhood integrity, and mobilize citizens to restore lost community? What is needed to rebuild civil society, diminish individualism, and restore manners and civility? Social movements are a key part of the answer. As sociologist David Poponoe says, "rather than ideological debates, what is needed is a new national resolve and an all-fronts mobilization."[10]

Possibilities for mobilizing social change lie in the areas of parental monitoring of entertainment content and the reducing of television's dominance, the restoration of manners, citizen action against crime and teen pregnancy, volunteer movements, and mentoring, to name several.

#4: THE RESTORATION OF FAMILY: THE CALL TO FATHERHOOD

America's deepening social crisis is primarily linked to the family, most specifically to the institution of fatherhood. Presently more than 15 million children are being raised in households in which the biological father is absent. This phenomenon largely explains the growing poverty, alienation, and dysfunction of our nation's young people. This trend, like others, will be reversed when the cultural message encourages the pursuit of adult self-fulfillment through, not apart from, children.

A growing body of research confirms what intuition and practical wisdom have long regarded as self-evident: fathers play an indispensable role in the cognitive and psychological development of children, in developing character and discipline, in forming healthy gender identification, and in a host of other personal factors. No public program, income transfer, or child-support payment will ever substitute the presence of a nurturing father. The father's role is non-exchangeable and irreplaceable.

Currently, about one-third of all American children live away from their biological fathers. Among the children of divorce, half have never visited their father's home. In a typical year, 40 percent of them do not see their father; 20 percent have not seen their father in five years.[11]

This unprecedented level of family disruption should be cause for great concern. Instead, according to Barbara Dafoe Whitehead, "the media depicts the married two-parent family as a source of pathology." And those who view the family crisis with alarm are dismissed as pessimists and nostalgists.[12]

Perhaps in no area have Americans engaged in a more deadly act of collective self-delusion than in suggesting that society can liberate itself from an institution so critical as family, particularly fatherhood. Nothing more explains the enveloping social dysfunction and escalating government programs than this notion of liberationism: that adults can advance their own agenda while speculating about the resilience of children.

If we are to make progress, all Americans need to confront family disintegration. The debate over family in America has become highly politicized. Many have all but implied that to be committed to the family, one must be a registered Republican, even though the real task of advancing strong families is non-political. As a basic and irreplaceable unit of society, the family is of too universal importance for it to be captured by partisan movements or desperate politicians. Responsible liberals must join responsible conservatives in forging a joint commitment family restoration.

Whatever else family debates include, they must have as their primary objective the restoration of the basic unit of the family. Everything else is secondary. Restoring parenthood does not require a return to women's social roles of the fifties, nor exclude men from family responsibility. Women's social and economic gains are not about to be reversed. But what must be reversed is the absence of fathers from their children. Up until the early nineteenth century, much of the child-nurturing responsibilities fell to men, and men met the challenge with confidence and pride.

Anthropologists have long observed the difficulty of socializing males in society, particularly if fathers are seen as superfluous. The consequence is not only the children's acute personal pain, but social and cultural disorder. U.S. Senator Daniel Patrick Moynihan has said, "A community that allows a large number of young men to grow up in broken families, dominated by women, never acquiring any stable relationship to male authority, never acquiring any set of rational expectations about the future—that community asks for and gets chaos." He has described the result as "a furious, unrestrained lashing out at the whole social structure" that is not only to be expected, but is "very near to inevitable."[13]

No reality should be more sobering for male Americans than the recognition of how many problems and sources of pain could be eliminated if men determined to change them—the physical and sexual abuse of children, sexual violence against women, poverty, pornography, and violence and crime, to name a few. All serious social problems in American are empirically tied to missing or dysfunctional fathers. Studies show, for example, that 70 percent of juveniles in correctional facilities are from fatherless households, and that fatherless children are five times more likely to live in poverty and twice as likely to drop out of school.

The greatest social problem in America is not "the family" but fatherhood. It is not women, after all, who are abandoning or neglecting their children. Men must come to recognize that fatherhood involves much more than a biological act; it is at least an eighteen-year economic obligation and preferably much more.

The time has come to launch a social movement that unreservedly promotes the virtue of responsible fatherhood. It must challenge the idea that it is macho to impregnate and not provide. The idea of abandoning one's flesh and blood to a life of significantly higher risk of emotional suffering and personal failure is a sign of deep personal weakness—not manliness. Culture once understood this, when the benefits of society, from good jobs to social status, were withheld from an adult male who was not "a good family man."

Now, to the detriment of America's children, the irresponsibility of an adult male is seen almost entirely as a private matter that has no public consequences and thus is beyond society's concern. A fatherhood movement could reattach social status and rewards to men for their upholding the importance of fatherhood. For fatherhood is a cultural institution and must be restored through cultural strategies. Fortunately, there are signs of renewed interest in the family that can be tapped to promote responsible fatherhood in the culture.

#5: THE RESTORATION OF FAITH: THE LIFE OF THE SPIRIT

This book concludes with a call to faith. Without faith, as the Scripture says, "it is impossible to please God." But without faith, it may also be impossible to enjoy personal peace and social order. Faith is, of course, the work of God, not of humans. But its restoration in American life will require that people recognize its need and seek it.

National strength is rooted in spiritual foundations. The founders were clear on this. John Adams wrote that the American Constitution was written for "a moral and religious people, and is wholly inadequate for the government of any other." The only real bulwark against a powerful state is a strong moral life. And George Washington said that a republic could not be maintained without a virtuous people. If private virtue failed, men and women would look to government for the things the people must do themselves if they wish to remain free.

Throughout the course of American history many have understood the link between America's economic success and her basic values. During the roaring twenties, Calvin Coolidge remarked: "We live in an age of science and abounding accumulation of material things. These did not create our declaration. Our declaration created them." Further, he said, "the things of the spirit come first." Coolidge said, "Unless we cling to that, all of our prosperity, overwhelming though it may appear, will turn to a barren sceptre in our grasp."

History's lessons suggests that an enduring freedom may be the exception to the rule. The most colorful chapters in history have been written by crusading dictators and unscrupulous democrats, not those who, like Washington and Lincoln, spent many hours on their knees seeking divine guidance for a nation that would conceive itself on freedom, not force.

This freedom to which the founders pledged their lives, fortunes, and sacred honor was not a freedom based on a series of abstractions devised by sophisticated calculators. It was a freedom born of the recognition of the providential care of a loving God who secures the rights of humans.

Decades-long efforts by secularist forces to stamp out religion's influence have failed; in fact it is secularism that faces exhaustion. Humans are spiritual beings. For example, seventy years of communist repression and the slaughter of millions did not destroy the souls of the living or the dead. It did destroy churches and synagogues and sent believers to psychiatric wards and dissidents to gulags. But no power on earth can crush the human spirit. Even after all of this oppression, government surveys found 30 percent of the people to be active believers.

Aleksandr Solzhenitsyn has written of his experience of living in a Stalinist labor camp. He was imprisoned for committing the state crime of writing about the tortures of Soviet prisons and psychiatric wards. It was on the rotting straw of the camp that he discovered the real meaning of freedom. "It was in my prison camp that for the first time I understood reality. It was there that I realized that the line between good and evil passes not between countries, not between political parties, not between classes, but down, straight down, each separate individual human heart."[14] True to its resurrection power, faith will always rise again.

Hardship can fortify and enrich faith. Solzhenitsyn found that the only response to absolute power was not an alternative form of power but finding freedom in divine love and forgiveness. A faith refined by that kind of fire is capable of shaking an entire nation.

Perhaps the proposition that God is dead was subjected to a more serious test in the West where a different kind of materialism—this one rooted in prosperity and moral indifference—exacted a deadly toll on the life of a people. In a tragic twist of irony, physical suffering may produce moral courage while prosperity and physical comforts produce boredom, complacency, and moral decay.

Solzhenitsyn wonders whether American ideals may be losing their hold on American hearts at the very moment of their triumph abroad. He said, "I could not recommend your society such as it is today as a model for the transformation of ours. Through intense spiritual suffering, our country has now achieved a spiritual development of such intensity that the Western system in its present state of spiritual exhaustion does not look attractive."[15]

If spiritual power was sufficiently strong to resist and eventually topple a totalitarian state, it should be more than sufficient in our struggle. For the greatest needs in America are for hope and healing. No political agenda, by itself, will significantly change aimless and estranged individuals. No agenda will, by itself, cause us to apply true compassion, seek true justice, or offer true repentance and healing. These are miracles that no government can perform. They are gifts of grace that come to those whose hearts have been changed.

The possibility of a return to the first things of faith, the "permanent things" upon which social order is based, stirs hope again of genuine national restoration. The turbulence of the times, an aging population, and economic and social dislocation all suggest that religious faith will be a growing factor in American life. As we face today's challenges, only such a return to the first things of faith can strengthen our resolve in the urgent task of restoring the good society.

NOTES

Chapter 1: The Search For America's Lost Soul

1. William Van Dusen Wishard, "The Cultural Context of a Sustainable Future" (Speech before World Business Academy, Dallas, Tex., 25 March 1993).
2. Irving Kristol, "The Coming Conservative Century," *Wall Street Journal*, 1 February 1993, p. A10.
3. Christopher Lasch, *The True and Only Heaven* (New York: Norton, 1991), p. 171.
4. David Walsh, *After Ideology* (San Francisco: Harper, 1990), p. 3.
5. Daniel Bell, *The Cultural Contradictions of Capitalism* (New York: Basic, 1976), p. xxix.
6. Robert Bellah, *Habits of the Heart* (New York: Harper & Row, 1985), p.15.
7. Robert Bellah, *The Good Society* (New York: Knopf, 1991), p. 5.
8. Tom Robbins quoted in John Kenneth White, *The New Politics of Old Values* (Hanover, Conn.: University Press of New England, 1990), p. 122.
9. Lasch, *The True and Only Heaven*, p. 22.
10. Ibid., p. 23.

Chapter 2: The Social Roots of America's Disorder

1. Barbara Dafoe Whitehead, "Dan Quayle Was Right," *Atlantic Monthly*, April 1993, p. 77.
2. Neal Peirce, "Filling our Prisons Isn't Deterring Crimes," *Philadelphia Inquirer*, 13 January 1992, p. A7.

3. U.S. Department of Health and Human Services, Division of Vital Statistics, Mortality Branch, February 1990.
4. William Raspberry, "Time for Blacks to Look Inward," *Washington Post*, 13 March 1992, p. A25.
5. *Beyond Rhetoric: A New American Agenda for Children and Families*, Report for the National Commission on Children (Washington, D.C.: U.S. Government Printing Office, 1991), p. 8.
6. Ibid., p. 67.
7. *Adolescent Sexuality, Pregnancy and Childbearing* (Washington, D.C.: The National Academy of Science, 1985), pp. 75–92.

Chapter 3: Culture and the Politics of Values

1. H. Richard Niebuhr, *Christ and Culture* (New York: Harper & Row, 1951), p. 33.
2. Christopher Scanlan, "Survey Finds Nearly One in Ten Youths Fired a Gun at Someone," *Philadelphia Inquirer*, 20 July 1993, p. 1.
3. See George Barna, *What Americans Believe* (Ventura, Calif.: Regal, 1991).

Chapter 4: Lessons from History

1. Richard John Neuhaus, "The Electoral Uses and Abuses of Religion," *First Things*, December 1992, p. 7.
2. Richard John Neuhaus, *The Naked Public Square* (Grand Rapids, Mich.: Eerdmans, 1984), p. 37.
3. See Sydney E. Ahlstrom, *A Religious History of the American People* (Garden City, N.Y.: Image Books, 1975).
4. Joel Hunter quoted in Michael Scott Horton, *Made In America: The Shaping of Modern American Evangelicalism* (Grand Rapids, Mich.: Baker, 1991), p. 17.
5. Leland Ryken, *Worldly Saints: The Puritans as They Really Were* (Grand Rapids, Mich.: Academic Books, 1986), p. 173.
6. Dean Curry, "Learning to Speak Anew: An Evangelical Reclamation of the Natural Law Tradition" (Paper prepared for the American Political Science Association, Chicago, Ill., September 1992), p. 10.
7. Quoted in "Diadalus," *The National Review*, 31 December 1985, p. 24.

Chapter 5: The Secular Heresy

1. Os Guinness, *The American Hour* (New York: Free Press, 1993), p. 20.
2. T. S. Eliot, *Christianity and Culture* (New York: Harvest/HBJ Books, 1977), p. 101.
3. Friedrich Nietzsche, *The Will to Power*, trans. Walter Kaufmann (New York: Random House, 1967), p. 3.
4. Russell Kirk, *The Roots of American Order* (Malibu: Calif.: Pepperdine University Press, 1977), p. 6.
5. Discussed in Russell Kirk, *The Politics of Prudence* (Bryn Mawr, Pa.: Intercollegiate Studies Institute, 1993), p. 28.
6. Arianna Stassimopoulos Huffington, *After REASON* (New York: Steim and Day, 1978), p. 3.
7. Ibid., p. 3.
8. Ibid., p. 10.
9. Edward R. Norman, "Freedom in an Age of Selfishness," *The Intercollegiate Review*, Spring 1993, p. 6.
10. Peter L. Berger, *A Far Glory: The Quest for Faith in an Age of Continuity* (New York: Free Press, 1992), p. 45.

Chapter 6: Secularism Unleashed

1. Philip E. Johnson, "Nihilism and the End of Law," *First Things*, March 1993, p. 19.
2. Ibid., p. 20.
3. Wishard, "The Cultural Context of a Sustainable Future," 25 March 1993.
4. Mark C. Henrie, "Rethinking American Conservatism in the 1990s: The Struggle Against Homogenization," *The Intercollegiate Review*, Spring 1993, p. 14.
5. Ibid., p. 37.
6. Kirk, *The Politics of Prudence*, p. 30.
7. Ronald H. Nash, *The Closing of The American Heart: What's Really Wrong with the American Heart* (Richardson, Tex.: Probe Books, 1990), p. 189.
8. Niebuhr, *Christ and Culture*, p. 37.
9. Paul C. Vitz, *Censorship: Evidence of Bias in Our Children's Textbooks* (Ann Arbor, Mich.: Servant, 1986), p. 91.

10. C. S. Lewis, *The Abolition of Man* (New York: Macmillan, 1947), p. 13.

Chapter 7: The Proper Role of Religion and Politics

1. Alexis de Tocqueville, *Democracy In America*, vol. I (New York: Vintage Books, 1945), p. 319.
2. Ibid., p. 315.
3. Ibid., p. 320.
4. Ibid., p. 322.
5. Ibid., p. 321.
6. Quoted in Richard John Neuhaus, *Doing Well and Doing Good: The Challenge to the Christian Capitalist* (New York: Doubleday, 1992), p. 48.
7. John Courtney Murray, "The Problem of Religious Freedom," *Theological Studies* 25 (1964): pp. 503–575.
8. Eliot, *Christianity and Culture*, p. 45.
9. Doug Bandow, "God and the Economy: Is Capitalism Moral?" *Terra Nova*, vol. 1, no. 4, 1992, p. 40.

Chapter 8: Four Personal Requirements

1. Quoted in "Diadalus," p. 27.
2. Quoted in "The Odyssey of a Religious Thinker," *Insight*, 17 February 1986, p. 74.
3. Jacques Ellul, *The Presence of the Kingdom* (Colorado Springs, Colo.: Helmers and Howard, 1989), p. 35.
4. Ibid., p. 16.
5. Ibid., p. xli
6. Guinness, *The American Hour*, p. 189.
7. See Martin Luther King, Jr.'s early sermon "The Transformed Nonconformist."
8. John Seel, "Nostalgia for the Lost Empire," in Os Guinness and John Seel, eds., *No God But God: Breaking With the Idols of Our Age* (Chicago: Moody, 1992), p. 66.
9. Walsh, *After Ideology*, p. 68.
10. John Courtney Murray, *We Hold These Truths: Catholic Reflections on the American Proposition* (New York: Sheed and Ward, 1960), pp. 11–12.

11. Dietrich Bonhoeffer, *The Cost of Discipleship* (New York: Macmillan, 1955), p. 23.

12. St. Augustine, *City of God*, Vernon Bourke, ed. (Garden City, N.Y.: Image Books, 1958), pp. 27–29.

13. Quoted in Joel C. Hunter, *Prayer, Politics and Power* (Wheaton, Ill.: Tyndale, 1988), p. 13.

14. See King, "The Transformed Nonconformist."

Chapter 9: Five Public Responsibilities

1. Richard John Neuhaus, "Putting First Things First," *First Things* no. 1 (March 1990), p. 7.

2. Christopher Dawson, *Beyond Politics* (Freeport, N.Y.: Books for Libraries, 1971), p. 21.

3. Ibid., p. 26.

4. Murray, *We Hold These Truths*, p. xi.

5. James Davison Hunter, *Culture Wars: The Struggle to Define America* (New York: Basic, 1990), p. 298.

6. Bonhoeffer, *The Cost of Discipleship*, p. 166.

7. Kirk, *The Politics of Prudence*, p. 1.

8. Ibid., p. 29.

9. Ibid., p. 31.

10. Walsh, *Beyond Ideology*, p. 18.

11. Dawson, *Beyond Politics*, p. 25.

12. J. Wesley Bready, *England: Before and After Wesley* (London: Hodder & Stoughton, 1939), p. 11.

13. Timothy L. Smith, *Revivalism and Reform: American Protestantism on the Eve of the Civil War* (Baltimore, Md.: Johns Hopkins University Press, 1980), p. 180.

14. Marvin Olasky, "Beyond the Stingy Welfare State," *Policy Review*, no. 54 (Fall 1990), p. 2.

15. Quoted in Mitchell Pearlstein, "When it Comes to Ills of Society, Two Economists take a Spiritual Approach," *Minneapolis City Business Journal*, 11 June 1993.

16. Quoted in James W. Skillen, ed., *Abraham Kuyper: The Problem of Poverty* (Grand Rapids, Mich.: Baker, 1991), p. 15.

Chapter 10: Renewing America's Civic Vision

1. George Gallup, *Forecast 2000* (New York: William Morrow, 1984), p. 11.
2. Walsh, *Beyond Ideology*, p. 265.
3. Quoted in Jonathan Elliot, ed., *Debates on the Adoption of the Federal Constitution* (New York: B. Franklin, 1988), p. 369.
4. Amtai Etzioni, *The Spirit of Community* (New York: Crown, 1993), p. 230.
5. James Q. Wilson, "The Contradictions of an Advanced Capitalist State," *Forbes*, 14 September 1992, pp. 110–116.
6. See Harry C. Boyte, *CommonWealth: A Return to Citizen Politics* (New York: Free Press, 1989).
7. William Raspberry, "Social Traps, Individual Effort," *Washington Post*, 4 March 1991, p. A13.
8. Michael Joyce, "Philanthropy and Citizenship," *Imprimis*, vol. 22, no. 5 (May 1993), p. 1.
9. Quoted in Russell Kirk, *The Conservative Mind From Burke to Eliot* (Chicago: Regnery, 1986), p. 17.
10. Ibid.
11. Quoted in Peter L. Berger and Richard John Neuhaus, *To Empower People: The Role of Mediating Structures in Public Policy* (Washington, D.C.: AEI Press, 1977), p. 4.
12. Ibid.
13. See Dawson, *Beyond Politics*.
14. Berger and Neuhaus, *To Empower People*, p. 6.
15. Joyce, "Philanthropy and Citizenship," p. 2.
16. Ibid.
17. Robert Nisbet, *The Quest for Community*, quoted in ibid., p. 3.
18. G. K. Chesterton, *What I Saw in America* (New York: Dodd Mead, 1922), p. 8.
19. Bell, *The Cultural Contradictions of Capitalism*, p. 83.

Chapter 11: Establishing the National Priorities

1. Bill Schambra, ed., *As Far As Republican Principles Will Admit* (Washington D.C.: AEI Press, 1992), p. 6.
2. Bell, *The Cultural Contradictions of Capitalism*, p. 70.
3. David Boaz, "School Reform was a Failure; Try Vouchers," *Insight*, 5 July 1992, p. 18.

4. Peter H. Gibbon, "In Search of Heroes, *Newsweek*, 18 January 1993, p. 9.

5. Lawrence W. Reed, "As Values Collapse, Government Grows," *Viewpoint*, The Makinac Center, 24 February 1992, no. 92–94, p. 1.

6. Ibid.

7. Ibid.

8. Quoted in Edward B. Fiske, "Parental Choice in Public School Gains," *New York Times*, 11 July 1988, p. B6.

9. David Blankenhorn, "Fatherless America" (Minneapolis: Center for the American Experiment, Policy Report, April 1993), p. 1.

10. David Popenoe, *Family Affairs*, The Institute for American Values, vol. 5, no. 1–2 (Summer 1992), p. 17.

11. Richard Weissbourd, "Trust Fund," *The New Republic*, 8 November 1992, p. 25.

12. Whitehead, "Dan Quayle was Right," p. 55.

13. Daniel Patrick Moynihan, "Help for Our Cities," Speech given to U.S. Senate (n.d.).

14. Aleksandr Solzhenitsyn, *The Gulag Archipelago* (New York: Harper & Row, 1973), p. 168.

15. Ronald Berman, ed., *Solzhenitsyn at Harvard* (Washington, D.C.: Ethics and Public Policy Center, 1976), p. 12.